MONSTERS:
Poetry on How to Bite Back

MW00334566

JACQUI SWIFT

Monsters: Poetry on How to Bite Back

Monsters: Poetry on how to Bite Back
Copyright© 2016 Jacquelyn Swift. No portion of this book may be reproduced mechanically, electronically, or by any other means including photocopying without written permission of the publisher. It is illegal to copy this book, post it on a website or distribute it by any other means without permission from the publisher.

Jswiftbooks.com
Jswiftbooks@gmailcom
Facebook: /JacquiSwiftbooks

Review me on Amazon!

Limits of Liability and disclaimer of warranty

The author and publisher shall not be liable for your misuse of this material. This book is strictly for informational and educational purposes.

Disclaimer
The purpose of this book is to educate and entertain. The author and publisher do not guarantee that anyone following these techniques, suggestions, tips, ideas, or strategies will become successful. The author and publisher shall have neither liability nor responsibility to anyone with respect to any loss or damage caused or alleged to be caused, directly or indirectly by the information contained in this book.

Edited by Shavonna Bush
Artwork and Cover by Loren Viera
Interior Design by Laura Brown

ISBN 9781941749524
Library of Congress Control Number: 2016947597

4-P Publishing
Chattanooga, TN

Acknowledgments

I would like to thank Laura Brown, 4-P Publishing, and The S.W.A.T. Book Camp for leading by example and helping me tap into the courage it takes to self-publish.

Thank you to my mentor Shavonna Bush and Benjamin Smith for reading, re-reading editing, encouraging, and helping with the overall launch of this project!

Thank you to Loren Viera for the beautiful cover and pictures within!

I want to thank my first Beta readers Bridgette Benford and Dr. Elizabeth Renneisen who were always up to date on my latest teenage fiction in high school!

Contents

Reader,

By no means must you read this book chronologically from chapters one to ten. Though I have arranged the information into a step-by-step guide, this is a multifunctional poetry/self-help guide all about your personal journey towards fighting off your hostile inner monsters (insecurity, depression, anxiety for example). Take what you need for your monster hunt. My chapters are named for the steps towards making a brunch of your own demons. I just want you to eat well.

This book contains real, bold, unapologetic thought on how to navigate life as an adult that is still dealing with the monsters in the closet you thought you had left at mama's house. If coarse language, uncomfortable situations, and a few volcanic eruptions of some cool poetry are going to bother you, treat this book like a green, slimy piece of cold cut ham and put it down quickly. Then go wash your hands.

If you want to take this ride with me, and have a good old fashioned monster barbecue, welcome!

Jacqui

CHAPTER 1: HUNT

People have always told us to face our demons. I say hunt them
down and eat them with a bit of salt and parsley for garnish.
Confronting a monster is great as a first step, but our goal should
be to eliminate, expel, and purify. This is how we modify ourselves
into becoming, better, stronger, more kickass people. To "hunt"
you must first acknowledge what monster is causing you internal
harm. More than likely whatever kind of monster you are dealing
with is holding you back from noticing sprigs of everyday joy you
could be taking advantage of in life.

"The Joy Hunt"

The act of living creatively, and the process of having a hand in creating your own joy precedes having the language to describe it. You don't go around verbalizing: *I want to be happy! I want to do something amazing! Someone tell me where to find the next train to Adventure-town!* It is about what people feel from you, and what your surroundings are picking up on in your behavior. Do you stay locked inside your daily routine? Same cereal, same route to work, same color shoes? Or do you walk off cliffs and hope for the best? Around every corner and beneath every rock on this planet is an adventure designed specifically for you. It is all here so that you may create your own joy from it by taking risks, and exploring.

We love saying things are "none of our business," but the entire world belongs to us and we to it. Everything is your business, and can be your potential happiness. The two most important tools a person should utilize in order to live imaginatively are sincerity and beauty. At a 2016 Slam Poetry Conference, I had the pleasure of meeting Amir Sulaiman, poet and activist. He refers to sincerity and beauty as the pillars a poet needs to understand his craft. Poetry is living art or the written art of living. Just being alive is the most honest and humble thing about a human, but sincerity requires courage and a willing sacrifice of pride. Humility is also a result of sincerity. When we present ourselves as we truly are, we can shed the comfort in illusion, and tap into reality which can be much more fascinating. The Poet does this to make his writing a livable, relatable home for his audience. One who lives creatively, however; does this in order to tear down the constructs of faux happiness, and get to the gravel path of sincere Joy.

Taking this one step further, illusion is valuable when it isn't being used as a front to keep up appearances for whatever reason. In fact, there is no real proof of the outside world. It is illusion by nature. Amir relays the unspeakable wonders of being human and interacting with our world through a question of the existence of an empty water bottle. He holds it up and asks us,

> **You are the universe as well as you are you.**

"How do you know that this bottle is real?"

The room grows swollen with mounds of scientific definitions of matter, arguments about the fact that he was holding it: *we can see it! It was once full, and now it is empty. Maybe it's not real, and we're dreaming! We're not dreaming clearly it's real because it just is.* Amir responds to the last commentator: Do you always know when you're dreaming? You may perceive it as real because you see it, but have your eyes never been fooled before?

Keeping in mind that we do not see with our eyes, but that our brains create the images from our outside world, we are left to conclude that we see the outside world inside of ourselves. That wide open sunset across the bridge from you is inside of you. Everything you hear, see, smell, touch, and experience all happens inside of you. To see is to experience an illusion. It is a reproduction of your brain. The only way to interact with matter is through sensory perception so Matter =

13

Illusion. Therefore, if you have heard it, seen it, or felt it....it happened inside of you.

All of this means that you are the universe and everything in it. Imagine this, there is a black hole known as J0100+2802 that is 1 billion times the mass of the sun. If we can witness something with that kind of mass, power, and age; it means something that powerful, ancient, and massive is inside of us. So then you have a responsibility. When living day to day, you are to present yourself as everything in the universe. You have to live as awakened as possible because with everything you interact with, you grow in size. You become greater by expanding and experiencing more because it happens inside of you.

You are the universe as well as you are you. So you actually have an advantage over everyone else. When are *you* ever going to happen again? There will never be

> **"Envy is ignorance and imitation is suicide"**

another you, and no one will ever know what it is like to be inside your expansion. You have a unique advantage point and a responsibility not to cover yourself up in trying to copy other universes you see.

"Envy is ignorance and imitation is suicide," says Amir, as he uses this analogy in his discussion: If we are all metaphors in this poem of existence, then the Great Poet has a specific job he wants us to do. If you are a part of line three, don't be jealous of line seven. Don't eliminate then impersonate line seven. If you do that, you will screw up the entire poem. If you refuse to be true to yourself and show your true self to the outside world, you are literally messing up the flow of the universe.

The second most important tool to living imaginatively is Beauty. Through words, the Poet exposes beauty in the ugliest situations. This supposes that beauty can be found even in ugly things. What if we could use that same mentality and expose the beauty in the ugliest times of our own lives? It takes courage to have your heart break, find something magnificent inside of it, and then look back and wonder: *who would ever want a heart that is unbroken or fixed in the first place?* To manifest courage you need danger, pain, or suffering. What we do with pain and suffering is our choice. All suffering can be connected to beauty as pain can be connected to growth. The Poet learns to read, feel, and translate pain until the pain becomes something that the audience knows they must bear in order to understand their own humanity. Understanding your own humanity; that is beauty.

All this to say a few things:

- Hunt for joy on the surface of your life as well as in the corners you never go into.
- Why mix poetry with self-help? Well, the poem and the human have as much in common as the Poet and God. The interesting thing about the human is that she can interchangeably be human, poem or Poet...what does that say about us? We are Divine. Self-help is a genre I believe should help you see yourself as you really are, and you are absolutely Divine.
- Beauty and Sincerity. Make it your life's work to figure out how to obtain and retain

15

those two things in order to live an overall more imaginative life.

Earlier I mentioned jumping off cliffs as a metaphor for taking risks. Let's pick up there. I jump off cliffs every day.

Exhlblt A.

I was a homeless hostel hopper in a country where I did not even recognize some of the characters in their alphabet. It was Oslo, Norway. I just wanted some cheesecake and maybe a prawn sandwich with Gjetost cheese on the side. My legs burned from walking the cobblestone sidewalks all day. I was there with a group but decided to go at things alone for a while. An our into it, I had begun to think I'd made a big mistake.

First of all, I'd left the hostel with only enough Kroner (money) to eat. What if I needed something else? There's a charge for grocery bags and ice water there. Who knows what I might have to have extra cash for?

No matter which way I turned my map the words still didn't make sense, but here I was, tourist Jacqui turning and turning that damn map like it would morph into something readable. You really shouldn't do that as you're walking down a heavily peopled sidewalk in the middle of Oslo. BAM!

The impact felt like I'd run into more than one person. I looked up and saw three people a little older than me. The two guys were twins, and the girl had on this fabulous red scarf with sequins at the bottom. Then

I noticed the person I knocked down on the ground beside me rubbing his elbow.

"I'm so sorry about that!" I said. By this time his group of friends were laughing.

"No worries, I should really make a habit of minding the front of me instead of chattering with these idiots." He smiled as we helped each other up. I learned they were also tourists out looking for something to eat while the rest of the travelers with them were sleeping in.

An hour later we had Poppy seed bread, raspberry jam, and tons of cheeses! Our adventure lasted until late that afternoon once we'd danced in the streets with a city performance group, I got kissed by an elderly French lady, the twins got in this violent break dancing battle, and we got rained on for an hour trying to get to the F Tram while laughing hysterically at the way the entire city was in fast forward trying to stay dry.

My stop was first. They walked me up the hill towards Oslo Vandrerhjem Haraldsheim (who's idea was it to build this hostel on a 90 degree hill?), and we said our reluctant goodbyes.

Do you often avoid situations that will get you lost even if you have time to find your way out of them? Quit that.

Exhibit B

At 17, his were the first arms I ever fell asleep in and woke up looking for. Joy for me during our time was us sitting in an almost telepathic silence on the steps of his porch listening in anticipation for the cicada's to stop hissing and be replaced by the lightening bugs.

17

As in tune and similar as we were, my love had a dangerous habit I didn't know about. He said it helped take him out of his head, away from all the stress senior year was piling on his shoulders. We had been an official couple for a year, and I wanted in on this stress reliever.

After school one Friday, I rode with him out to the edges of the city to our favorite bridge. Instead of walking across it to get to that clearing where the Marigolds bloomed next to the lake, we stopped in the center of the bridge. It always freaked me out because the bridge spanned over about a 100ft. drop down into the river with the jagged rock, and the fish with teeth.

"Babe, what the hell?!" I screech as I watched him crawl up onto the metal ledge and hold on to one of the erect poles on the bridge's side; Taking a deep breath, he let go and closed his eyes. I thought my heart was going to collapse.

"When I'm up here, everything else gets smaller. My grades are perfect, my dad's not sick, you and I end up at the same college, and there's nothing to worry about because my entire life becomes this ledge." He said this with a quiet conviction that made me wonder if he'd ever considered jumping. The wind started up, and I couldn't keep the tear from falling down my cheek.

"Please get down from there." I pled in attempted calmness.

"You come up." He retorted like he was offended at the suggestion.

"This isn't funny. You could fall!" I growled.

"And none of the stuff I mentioned would be an issue anymore...would it?" He swayed forward, and I almost retched. I stalked off the bridge toward the clearing furiously wiping my face. After about a half hour of lying on the grass thinking about what future we could possibly have together after this, I felt his shadow blocking my line of sun.

"Are you suicidal?" I asked opening one eye.

Saying nothing, he extended his hand to me. I don't know why I accepted it. I don't know why I walked back to the center of the bridge with him, and I don't know why the hell I let him lift me onto the same ledge he'd just been standing. I trembled like the ground was shaking.

"Look down." He insisted. When I did...that was all it took for me to understand what he was talking about. Though he had a grip on me and I had a grip on the bridge, I felt small, vulnerable, and scared of things that really mattered such as not falling to a slow liquid death. Everything else was "smaller" as he said. I'm not advocating this method of putting your life into perspective...a simple session of yoga meditation or mountain climbing should do the trick.

He could have pushed me off. I could have been clumsy and fallen myself. When he got up there with me once I'd gotten used to the feeling, we could have taken each other down Romeo and Juliet style. Risks like this may be strangely fulfilling, but it's important to identify if your adventures are giving you joy or feeding your monsters. We don't want to do that! Take risks, fall into all the love you can, but just being careful and remember the mission. The mission is not to find things that make you feel small in order to distract you from your monsters. It is to confront, cook, and consume your monsters through focus.

19

Exhibit C: Paulo Coelho

"It's something prohibited. Glasses are not purposely broken. In a restaurant or in our home we're careful not to place glasses by the edge of a table. Our universe requires that we avoid letting glasses fall to the floor. But when we break them by accident, we realize that it's not very serious. The waiter says it's nothing, and when has anyone been charged for a broken glass? Breaking glasses is a part of life and does no damage to us, to the restaurant, or anyone else. I bumped the table. The glass shook but didn't fall."

Paulo Coelho, writer of *The Alchemist*, said this through the mouth of his protagonist, Pilar, in *By the River Piedra I Sat Down and Wept*. This is a coming of age novel thematically centered upon testing boundaries and breaking out of the glass prison we put ourselves in when we put preconceived limits on our potential, curiosity, and desires. Those inhibitions are similar to this universally unspoken voice that tells us not to break things on purpose.

Armed with this metaphor, we are forced to consider if brokenness is a negative or a positive thing. When something is broken, after trying to figure out how to fix it, do we not use our critical thinking caps to try to figure out how to prevent the next crash? In this period of heightened thought, we tend to grow by finding flaws with our previous way of thinking which led to the breaking in the first place. This growth is our evolution from break to break to break. Brokenness is a part of evolution; it is a positive thing.

For many artists, breaking things is where the integrity of their craft lies. It's about going there and getting dirty with the mud of the earth and your own beautiful filth in the process. It's about jumping off things knowing damn well you can't fly but not being afraid of the fall because you know that your broken bones will make bread for you later, and you will never starve from being your lovely uninhibited self.

> **Use common sense, but don't put it in overdrive.**

Pilar says: "Break the glass, please and free us from all these damned rules! From needing to find an explanation for everything, from doing what others approve of...our parents taught us to be careful with glasses and with our bodies. They taught us that the passions of childhood are impossible, that we should not flee from priests, that people cannot perform miracles, and that no one leaves on a journey without knowing where they are going."

Why not find a journey and erase all notions of direction, space, the science of time, the arithmetic of logic...and just go. Try to find new ways to expand the way you understand your space. Where does that road lead? Well, let's drive down it and see. Oh, what? A frozen yogurt and jazz café?! Who knew this was here?? Not us if we hadn't taken the risk of getting lost and turned down this weird street.

Use common sense, but don't put it in overdrive. That shit will age you and make you feel 40 at 25. There are so many arbitrary rules we impose upon our own lives and the boundaries we build around ourselves as if we're trying to keep all our internal sheep safe in a

21

stable. Free the animals! Elizabeth Gibert, author of *Eat Pray Love*, would call it the *Big Magic*. Those more conscious then I would call it "being awake." I just call it opening up your joy and taking a piece out for the day. Have a peace of joy today.

The She Spirit

There are angels everywHERE.
 "Hey you!

You are fly
Now go do what you are before it's too late."

I had to keep repeating this as she walked towards the
ledge...

Looking over the edge about to fall to her death.

"There are angels everywHERE...guardians you can't
see."

When she heard me, she knew it was her own voice
with which I spoke.

The inner GOD-IS was rafting in the currents of her
blood. It was dancing to tribal rhythms in her pulse.

She had eyes like two turntables, and he was the DJ,
she forgot how to act when his music was at play.

"SIMPLIFY!" Said I,

"It's spring time, sweating actually makes you cooler.
'Sweating' others does not."

But it was too late...any dignity left in those small hands of hers was tapped out her fingertips in that last letter she wrote to her affections saying,

Dear love, I'm in you. You have me.
 Now do with me what you will. I surrender.

Sir, you render me breathless like the fear of drowning in the Baltic.

You loved like an empty canteen. No quench or life in you just air,

You loved bereft...and just out of reach.

I'd become a barefoot, dry skinned thick tongued woman...until I told all my dehydration to drown. Amen.

Only a father's love could soothe these wounds. The inner GOD-IS prayed...and wept...and prayed....and screamed and where there

Was once sand,

Rivers appeared.

The Earth sprouted greenery and cornfields bending beneath our bare backs.

Me, she, and GOD we marveled at the sky, painted ceilings of the planet

24

and breathed in together.
We lay there with our souls laid bare
We became the star-strewn sky.
"Simplify!" said I
And we floated... a glittery death awake.
No love no hate
No hurt just Earth.

CHAPTER 2:
INTIMIDATE

So you've got it in front of you, the evil thing that has been eating you up inside ever since the night of the situation that's haunting you. This monster is huge. It has influenced many of your decisions and emotions since its conception. It has kept you from breaking out of your box and seeking happiness. By unleashing your magic, taking risks, and embracing adventure you've managed to enter into a staring battle with the ungodly beast. Your eyes are full and feral as you've learned how to tap into your joy. This monster recognizes your independence and may begin to shrink.

"Fear"

If monsters can be frightened, then you know the power of fear can be inescapable sometimes. Fear sounds like siren noises in place of musical notes that play behind the repeated word "wait!" or "stop!"

I am afraid of everything. Holding it together is a perfected art that I've just gotten kind of good at. Do you remember the very first thing you were afraid of? Surely it wasn't failure, or debt, or pubic speaking just yet. As a child, what made you reach for your caretaker and hold on for dear life?

There is a fine line between fear and phobia. We can make the distinction of being afraid of heights and being an Acrophobic. People who are afraid of heights don't enjoy the feeling of being so far above the ground and find it best to limit situations in their lives that would take them skyward. An acrophobic, however, may rearrange their entire careers if it meant having to take an airplane flight. Rationality isn't everything, but it can be our best faculty against insanity and isolation. Reason can separate a perception of real danger and a false danger.

I have Emetophobia. This is the crippling fear of vomiting. Even though 20 percent of American's suffer from Emetophobia or some kind of anxiety disorder, Emets continue to struggle in communicating their fear to those closest to them who don't understand. There is not a single period of fifteen minutes that passes by in which people with this phobia are not thinking about the next time they may vomit, and how they can prevent it. Even if it's been over ten years since they were last sick.

Mine began from a traumatic viral experience when I was only five years old. After scaring my whole family, missing a week of school, and almost ending up in the emergency room; every twinge of nausea since then has reduced me to a debilitating panic.

Winters are the hardest because of Norovirus. This is the sickness that has its victims doubled over in gastric distress anywhere from 12-48 hours at a time. It's the sickness that everyone seems to have a story or two about and people tend to try to outdo the last person's description of how violently everything they'd eaten that day revisited them. (For those of us that keep our anxiety a secret this is UNBEARABLE to listen to. STOP IT.) Every year Norovirus causes 19 million to 21 million illnesses in the U.S, and it kills me to type that when it's known that the way to kill the virus and stop spreading it is to simply wash your hands with soap and water.

There was a horrible outbreak the winter of 2014 in the Middle Tennessee area. The online support group I am a part of was flooded with panic attacks in progress. Young adults were refusing to leave their dorm rooms or walk into public restrooms, parents of young children were feeling like crap for not being able to be in the same room with their vomiting child, teenagers were worried they'd contracted the illness due to one of their classmates vomiting in front of them at school. This phobia doesn't discriminate.

During this outbreak, I went to work the night shift at my job, only to find every Emetophobic's nightmare.

The worker I was relieving was retching behind the front desk. After she had left, when I tell you I did not touch a single thing at that front desk... I mean I took no phone calls, I didn't use the computer, no pens, no anything. I sat in the very front room, and if people came in needing assistance, I helped them from there the best I could. I was just trying to make it through the shift without a second bout of hyperventilating. I knew you couldn't catch it by breathing it in unless the infected fluids were near you, but I was still trying really hard not to breathe too deeply. I didn't dare go into the bathroom.

The root of suffering from this particular phobia comes from the fact that Emetophobics are afraid of something internal. Our fear comes from the inside of our own bodies, and the thing we are afraid of is uncontrollable. How do you console someone who is afraid of the irrational? You think you're being helpful by saying things like,

"Hey it happens to everyone, you can't die from it."

"You know it's going to happen eventually so why don't you just get over it?"

"No one likes to be sick you know."

"What will you do when you have kids? Think of them and it will cure you."

The thing these phrases lack is the understanding that a Phobia is not something you can rationalize away. These phrases lack sensitivity to what it means to have an anxiety disorder.

This can apply to talking to someone with any number of phobias. Whether it's a fear of clowns, dogs, heights, or closed in spaces; when comforting a person the first step is to attempt to understand fully what it's like to be them and to be afraid of what makes them afraid. No matter how strange, irrational, or insignificant you may feel their fear is, as the comforter, you put that aside and listen. Reassure. Practice self-restraint on your own opinion. What inconvenience is it to you to refrain from making the person feel like their fear is crazy?

If you don't know what to say, just listen and be present. No one expects you to be a psychologist. Sometimes it's just about being that person who can distract us long enough so that our breathing can stabilize after the panic attack. Moral of this story? Be a respirator, you guys.

Yes, the idea of carrying a child to term scares me more than anything (I'm attempting it for my new husband, but every time I think about it, I kind of want to shrivel up in a corner and die). Yes, I still have guidelines; no touching my face or mouth once I leave home, no eating finger foods from an event in the breakroom, no buffets, no roller coasters, very little alcohol, with finger foods I don't eat the part my fingers have touched. Yes, I still have rituals;

> **Remember. Your fear is not your god**.

lather hands four times before final rinse and dry, shower to the duration of four full Beyoncé songs if exposed to highly germy situations, Tums or Pepto before bed, two mints before and after each meal (mints keep queasiness away).

Sometimes you don't even realize you're making progress until that one little thing you used to do to protect yourself is no longer a part of your routine. We are all in the process of slowly healing one step at a time. The only difference between me now and me back when I was too scared to eat any more than soup and saltines every day is that now I acknowledge my fear is not my ruler nor does it define me.

Remember. Your fear is not your god. Your fear is smaller than you are. Your fear is your brain trying to protect you. If you do not need to be protected from the thing that it is alerting you about, you have got to consider ways to tone down the sirens.

Sirens may include: Panic attacks, shaking, sweating, hyperventilating, uncontrollable crying, avoiding everyday life situations, not eating, overeating, and locking yourself in your house for days. To tone these down, handle them individually. Progress is a result of freedom from internal chaos. Coping calmly with the smaller things: anxiety over lost papers, nervousness over feeling queasy, fear of saying a speech in front of a small group of people, is the first step to mastering a more well-adjusted you. The goal isn't perfection as much as it is getting the Monster of Fear to shrink smaller and smaller until you can put him in a cage like a pet canary and function like you want to.

Bathroom Floor

I know bars like trap doors and closed minds
Minds that hang traps over doors to freedom
Doors that trap minds into dead ends
Dead ends that force a free mind back into itself
I know a self that doesn't like herself
Can't stand the short shelf life of being okay
Once one day expired
I can't use it

Malleable

Just one dark alley away
One death
One new
found love
turned hate
turned love
again
One human
trafficker
One strange
phone call in
the night
One severe
panic attack

One cab ride gone wrong
One medical discovery
One stolen car
One brawl
One stripper pole
One failed semester
One wrong pill
One birth
away from a different life
We are all Gumby

CHAPTER 3: BITE

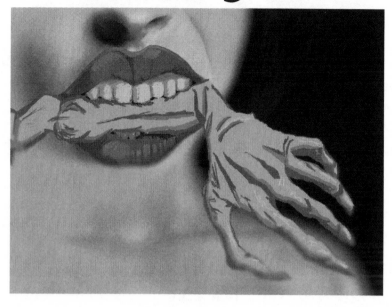

So you didn't let that monster scare you off. You stared it down to its core, peered deep into its origins. You stared it down so ferociously that you hypnotized it into stillness. Now you are close enough to BITE! Yes, your teeth are plenty sharp enough. Yes, you are stronger than you think! You are fierce, and your humanness has the divine power to protect itself. Do you dare wake the beast and start this fight with it? It's going to resist you. It is going to claw at your jugular and snap at your eyes. Are you ready for your first encounter with this thing you've tried to shove into your closet behind the skeletons?

"Pain and Other Things that Hurt"

Never let anyone take you somewhere you don't want to be. Even if it's just down the street and around the corner to the nearest little petty bad mood swing. No one should be able to brighten or dim your light without your permission. The type of manipulation that goes on in a soulmate based, committed relationship surpasses that of even the most seductive of seductresses, the most cultish of cults, and the most charismatic of salesmen. It's like two people swimming in a kiddie pool and one pees.

You're both going to be in a bad mood, and you're both going to have to shower. Not just the one who peed... BOTH of you. Then after the shower, you may start to think,

"Hmmm...didn't he think of how his little accident would affect me? Did he ever once consider how I might feel about having someone else's urine on me? How could he be so insensitive? Now I smell, and I'm upset, and he doesn't care because he's the one that caused it!"

Even though it's easy to make those kind of assumptions when on a roll down the hill of disappointment in your significant other, if we were to flip those thoughts around, perhaps we would find that the act of being upset with our spouse may be just as unrighteous as whatever they did to you.

What might have caused his accident? It was likely just an accident after all. Perhaps too much tea, or maybe something more serious that he may need to seek help for. I screamed and slapped him across the face when it happened. Was that the appropriate way to handle that even after he said, "Whoops…sorry." How did my insensitivity affect him?

Big fights and big issues are different monsters to battle when they happen. To build up the strength to confront them, the small things must be effectively smoothed over so you can continue to grow with each other and become strong enough to lean on each other when you need to.

All this to say that there are two types of pain in the kiddie pool analogy. There's peeing in the kiddie pool type of pain, and someone coming up and draining the damn thing dry until you feel the sharp rocks in the yard type of pain. My father drained the pool by being absent for patches of my life. He was a wonderful friend when he was around in my childhood, but a new girlfriend meant I became like his side-chick, put to the side until they were having problems, then he'd start coming around to see me again.

My theory is that I get so petty and angry over my husband peeing in the pool a little bit because my daddy kept draining my clean water when I was younger. A girl tends to search for emotional security and outward male validation more when this happens.

What can you do when something painful in your childhood negatively influences your adult behavior?

First, respect your ability to realize you're letting your past screw up your present.

Find a way to forgive your past and accept the reality of what happened. Understand your lack of control over it at the time and the fact that you now have the power to stop it from hurting you ever again.

Search for ways to protect your positive views on family without referencing the bad things that happened in yours.

Ntozake Shange's "For Colored Girls Who Have Considered Suicide" includes a monologue featuring the "Lady in Green" who's just been robbed of the things she liked best about herself. The thief was a lover in her case. Who is your thief?

What in life took the peeled upside down arc of your smile and bled it dry? What hid your laugh from you and turned you into some "simple bitch with a bad attitude?" How long has it been since you looked in the mirror and mourned for the you you were when you were capable of not being swallowed by your grief or anxiety from the moment you woke up until the hour you lay back down to toss and turn? It doesn't have to be this way.

Our pain, whether it be emotional, financial, physical, mental, or petty is something we need not be so quick to kick out of out of our houses.

Recognize that we can't be hurt on the inside from outside elements. It is our response to the outside aggravation that bothers us. If you feel aggravated, consider if it isn't your judgment of the incident that is actually aggravating you. I could not control whether my father was present or not, but I can choose whether I'm going cry about it or if I'm going to consciously beat the hell out of the stigma attached to girls with "daddy issues." I can choose to either end up in a string of relationships with part-time men like him, or I can distract myself from that emptiness in my life and go get a degree, or save a bunch of children from a burning bus or something.

The things within you are the only things you can control. Upon understanding that you literally have no control over anything, you'll be able to embrace the freedom in disregard. A healthy dose of not giving a fuck every now and then, and you won't find yourself in a state of low self-esteem or bitterness as you compare your situation to that of others.

Give up the illusion that things are supposed to be fair. Making eye contact with the blatant favoritism fate plays with human beings is the first step in accepting it.

And last, before this gets too preachy, the fear of death is useless. Averting your eyes from grief, death, or anything icky is dangerous. The key is to ebb your pain back towards the hole it came out of using your sense of freedom. Freedom from false hope, freedom from expectations, freedom from illusion. Wakefulness in a sense. Being awake in this way is the opposite of useless suffering. So wake up and smack that pain monster in the face.

House of Pain

I was making breakfast. Pain called me into the living room

Since we'd been living together, I learned to love him like he was human

He was sitting on the rug by the fire

"Come," he said using my ex's voice

(He swore he never did that on purpose)

When I approached him, he smiled and grabbed me

His fingers pressing bruises into my wrists

We stood and waltzed to a Vivaldi concerto for a long time

I relaxed into his grip and for a moment I was a china doll

So fragile and breakable that

my existence was a grace

The dance ended with me faced away from him

His grip sharpened

"Look into that glow. It is hot. It is fire. It is real."

I screamed as he forced my hand into the fireplace

I begged.

My pleas held no weight against his stone wall

My flesh bubbled, and in my thrashing

His soft laughter bounced off my back

I smelled myself cooking

And I was sure I would die.

Finally, he let my arm go and sighed in our communal silence

Then Pain said,

"it will heal."

Captivity

The captives have suffered ill-treatment
They've been forced into submission
And placed at the mercy of their enemies

So I challenge you
Listener

Look upon their tired shapeless faces in the shadow of the summer
And take pity.
Look at these fallen royal families
All scarred and wearing their skin like sackcloth
Hung loosely on their coat rack skeletons

Have you ever been there?
Have you ever been to the other side of joy?
Heard a belly laugh in reverse
In the place where darkness impersonates the light?
There is only night here.
The captives huddle tightly knit to each other's bodies
Chaining their bruised arms
trying their best not to be afraid
but the enemies can see they tremble
for that, they will be mercilessly punished

Listener...surely you've been here
Maybe you too have once been gripped against your will
once

Forced to worship enemy gods and suffer their orders
Gods with names like Pain, Lust, Jealousy, Wrath, Fear, Addiction,
The captives are only human
To be a captive is to be human

44

Which enemy tricked you into being a slave?
how did you escape?

Support the souls that fall victim
And tell them Liberty will come
Perhaps you too reside in the camp
Comfort the person next to you
Liberty is near
Suffering may remain for a night
For here it is always night
But rejoicing comes in the morning
Throw your shackles into the sun's mouth
And watch the iron clad oppression melt
May all dehydration drown
In the Missouri rivers, we'll wade in

The rain, in its wet shine, will wash away all doubt
We will run
And when we become tired
We will walk and when we ache
We will crawl, and when our knees are cut we will rest
And then get up and crawl again until we are able to walk
We will absorb the blows of the enemy
With our faces, eyes, and jaws
Then we will smile chipped tooth smiles as we persist
In the escape
it is written
There will be liberty for the captives

Anatomy of an Ache

You and I have learned to live somewhat peacefully
together
Pain.
We are concrete effigies that stand honoring gravity.
Tangible representations of the God's adjustments to
the imperfect.
Pain, let us drown together in the rain.
Eulogizing our desert skin,
lets you and I strip down to our skeletons and play
under Haitian volcanoes
Welcoming the fire to come teach our joints to burn.
We will ache the sunset into shades of red,
and pretend it was an accident

You are an unwelcome dinner guest,
and I haven't enough bread to break with you
So we'll starve together

under the smells of our neighbor's feasts and wine.
We will thirst before unshared fruits as nothing but
wind passes our lips.
We understand each other.
You force humility into my chest

I'll pray with you
Under a machete blade cleanly positioned at my
collarbone
Knelt in a patch of rusted nails

I'll pray for you

To end
Tied to the enemy's interrogation chair
Like a skyscraper standing against a suicidal morning

I'll pray with you
before the time bomb makes its last tick and we go
down screaming.

And on those self-inflicted days
When lack of wisdom and judgment locks us up
together
Pain...I trust you to teach me
We've thrown ourselves out of windows
And felt every shard of glass bleeding our bodies
mosaic
But the tragedy was useful
because we learned to stop jumping without wings.
Pain,
The web of a love's betrayal left you and I naked in
each other's arms
And I cursed you for your nature
Especially when you told me a "love" that betrays is an
oxymoron
You didn't mind when I screamed.
You hit me when I tried to wipe the tears.
You choked me when I tried to run back to him and
said,
"There is something better for you in the other
direction. Why don't you come?"

I realize now...we were meant to be tired old friends
The kind that take fishing trips too damn early in the
morning

47

And ride taxi cabs to city limits at night
Just to see how far they can get before they no longer
know where they are

I respect you
And no matter how many tear stained pillows we share
And how much darkness surrounds us
I will never go "heartless" or "pokerfaced."
I will smile through missing teeth
And curl up, homeless, on park benches in the winter.
I'll write you lullabies to sing off key
So I'll hear you coming.

Indigo Bars

I love the way it feels like the world is about to end
when an earthquake shakes the afternoon
The way that sudden surge of urgency kicks us into
fight or flight
I love the colors
That paint their way into the pockets of our mind
when we think of heaven
Gives me hope that even though the world is
disposable
And ends often
My mind will always innately construct something
beautiful to trail after it.

I was screaming when I wrote this
Soul sucking myself into a psychiatric corner of my
room
My wounds are made of those rainbows
That always seem to appear right at the signs of the
apocalypse
Coloring my insides like strobe lights and silence
He colored me violet
violent
When he forced my rainbow to submit to the whim of
his storms
He is a tornado...his hands, the splintered debris that
carries disease wherever it goes
I didn't want to be human that night
I wanted to be something bigger
With nails and teeth...something sharp and tall with a
tail and fire breath
I wanted to be death

So that when he kissed me he'd open his eyes and
Satan would be staring him in the face

His animal groans reminded me of what hell might
sound like
And his breath...the sulfur of warm Gin mixed with
sweat
I've never seen a shadow so dark
When it was done, it wiped its face and said, "see ya."
As would an acquaintance after a movie date
After our movie date, he was supposed to drop me off
at home
But somehow I ended up in that gray ally
This graveyard of broken glass and molded trash
This is what I've been reduced to
brown woman, stumbling around under a pitch black
night,
trying to find her way to her beige apartments
praying there won't be another of its species waiting in
the bushes
for a woman walking alone at night...

I planned his murder in a red notebook
On a blue and white bus
Same color as my shower curtains
The ones that watched as I washed the skin off my
bones
Scrubbed for hours after they examined me,
I heard the demons hitting the drain;
the splash sounded silver and clean
But I wanted acid...bleach... something anything to
strip this taste from my flesh

All seven of my rainbows colors stained a ring around
the tub

1...they never found him. Apparently, he wasn't even a
student.
2...I'm afraid to be alone...and I never go out at night
3...I want to go home. But my family is counting on me
to be the first to make it through these four years for
this degree. I'll need it for the career that's going to
help pay off these loans
4...the entire campus knows, I was the Campus alert
that morning and the example that everyone should
"be cautious with people you hang around, and to
report any suspicious activity" blood sacrifice and
lesson learned for them I guess.
5...they say it was my fault. I asked for it. How could
the dumb bitch not have known he wasn't a student
but a rapist
6...therapy only helps when I get a goody bag...student
health knows me by name
7...my lab partner looks just like him...

and I still have that red notebook with his death
painted on the inside.
I write my lab notes in it now
I want to be strong. Want a lions mane and a voice
that proves I belong to a kingdom
I want to forgive...and I want to arc my smile to the
bottom of the sun
And be golden like all those women in the books, and
on the talk shows
Who survived
In America, every two minutes, a woman is added to

this family of victims
But I don't want to be a victim
I want to be a soldier, not a damn captive
I want to help others like me and be socially active
demons work well in dark places
I want to force my fears into the light,
Stop hiding behind bitterness that there's no justice in
sight

But I'm not that strong though
and...earthquakes prepare us for fight or flight
And the apocalypse massages
bright...violent...murderous, vengeful
Colors
Into the mind of those who sense it coming
My world ended at the hands of a man that looks just
like this guy I do my lab homework with
So Later...when I sit behind the indigo bars...in a
faded beige jumpsuit
They'll ask me why I did it.
I saw the face of that shadow in him
He needed to see the rainbow

Daddy

Aug 19, 2015

I'll tell people about the boat.

You never saw it coming, and somewhere in the distance the lighthouse was getting lost in the fog all horror scenes seem to be draped with.

I'll tell them it was instant. Your blood was quickly swallowed down the throat of the sea and her mammals... so no one suffered.

I will make you seem brave. Nobel even... as I paint pictures, fairy tales, tall tales fabled in the dark of a stormy night where you battened down hatches, shouted captain's orders and won lots of treasure you would have brought us back as a gift.

When you returned on that ship...
If only you could have come back.
You see convoluting these frescos of colorful death and an honorable exit for you
From this life to the next
is a coping mechanism I learned somewhere in the 23 years of my life you let sail past you in your lifeboat of excuses.

Daughters and donuts at my elementary school 1999,

My Daddy's a diabetic, and if he even smells sugar, he turns blue and passes out. Yes, it's quite inconvenient for him. No, he can't even go into the candy isle in the grocery store. Nope, no sweets in our house. As a matter of fact, I don't think I want any doughnuts today after all.

Field trips in kindergarten

53

Zoo—

If daddy even sees an elephant, he will swell up like a walrus and flop around until he hurts himself. I get embarrassed so I told him not to come cuz I knew elephants were going to be here. Monkeys too, oh man if dad even sees a monkey he goes bananas...I think he's allergic to both. Either way no, he's not coming.

Museum

Art makes my daddy cry, but don't tell anyone I told you. He used to be a famous artist, but after his ear got cut off in a painting accident, they asked him to make something pretty to go inside this big church in Italy...but he couldn't hear so instead of painting the "bowl of fruit" they asked for, he painted a picture of a "bowl of soup". He got fired and now we live in a box. He hates art museums because they remind him of why we live in a box.

Until the excuses for you got more serious, the lies were enormous

The day after daddy daughter dance 2005 middle school

Yeah, my dad and I had a huge fight last night so I couldn't make it. He had the nerve to tell me I couldn't see Brian anymore! Can you believe that? I wasn't having that! God, he just cares too damn much and doesn't want me to grow up or have a life at all. I wish he'd just shut up and leave me alone. Aren't overbearing dads the worst??? If anyone knows about overbearing dad's, it's me.

Okay, I may have gone overboard at my first poetry award show when they asked both my parents to stand on either side of me as we took pictures of me accepting it. The year, 2000 (this was that weird stage when I discovered makeup and trained myself to talk tough like the girls on gangster TV shows did)

Yeah this is my moms, my pops recently joined some kind of circus. Nah chill with all that laughing cuz, I know what it sounds like but it's actually nothing to laugh about. The boot camp part is like a camp for clowns, bearded ladies, lions, tigers, bears, and even elephants. And yo, my dad is mad scared of elephants, swells up and starts flopping around like he's jonesing for a fix or something. They make you eat fire, and wake you up every three hours with a pie to the face until you can ride a unicycle while juggling pins all the way around the stinkin' arena. That's wack, right? Yeah I know, they trippin'. But this award, though! Yo big ups to sidewalks for keeping me off the streets and shout out to my famz for believing in me!

The first time I killed my father was at high school graduation.

My father was a brave soldier who gave his life for a purpose and is spiritually watching over us at this very moment, if you are quiet you can hear the rustle of reeds parting to make room for his large ghost feet, walking hard like an angel dad should.

You were a helluva guy at my college graduation

My father was the pilot on flight 165 from Nashville to Detroit. You know...the one that crashed into the Lake? There were 28 survivors because of his quick wits; I get that from him you know. This diploma I have to show is proof of the brains and veins of genius that run through my blood. I guess I get it from him.

So now...2015...marriage.

55

I got the standard text I was expecting but knew was not going to actually fucking come. For once, I knew I would not have to explain the recurring lack of your presence to a sea of inquiring faces as they look from me to the beautiful, elder version of me and the empty space next to her. Woman plus dead air equals baby girl? No that can't be, right? Babygirl...where's your dad? We want to get him in a nice family wedding picture. Who's walking you down the aisle? Oh, your old man must be so proud that you're doing this the right way...where's he at so I can shake his hand...I'm just preparing myself.

This time, you were in the Navy.

And I will tell them about the boat.

You never saw it coming, and somewhere in the distance the lighthouse was getting lost in the fog all horror scenes seem to be draped with.

I'll tell them it was quick, and the blood was immediately swallowed down the throat of the sea and her mammals... so no one suffered.

I will make you seem brave. Nobel even, as I paint pictures, fairy tales, tall tell tales fabled in the dark of a stormy night where you battened down hatches, shouted captain's orders and won lots of treasure you would have brought us back as a gift.

When you returned on that ship...

But.... later...when my baby boy or girl sees you on a random photograph and asks...

I just may tell them the truth.

CHAPTER 4: FIGHT

And so the confrontation has begun! How are you feeling? Round one baby, you've injured this ugly thing by biting him while he was stunned but now he is awake, angry, and coming right at you! He's got a lot of arms. This is just like how our painful memories and grudges have the tendency to attack us from every avenue of consciousness. You turn your head, and there it is, you spin around, and it's got you by the throat, you try to dodge, and it picks you up and throws you across the floor. What does it take to fight our regrets? Our shortcomings? Things that haunt us from the past? How can we gain enough confidence to punch all those things in the face and enjoy a nice dip in the pool afterward to get all the bad blood off? Better yet, how do we get enough

CONFIDENCE to just live our lives presently the way we want to live them? To be secure enough to say what we mean and mean what we say unapologetically? You've got some time to figure it out. You're putting up one hell of a fight so far.

"End Your Insecurity"

SCREAM. No, really it's a good exercise. Do it right now. If you're reading in public, give us a good internal guttural yell. There now, doesn't that feel better?

Sometimes it's hard to not want to claw your way out of your own skin if only to let the world know what you're really thinking before it's too late:

"Hey, I'm not okay with that."

"You've misunderstood me."

"I think you're taking advantage of me."

"You can't talk to me that way."

"I don't like that idea...NO"

"I asked for chocolate, not vanilla."

"Get away and never speak to me again."

"Piss off."

What do you say to yourself on a daily basis that you've wanted/needed to say out loud, but it just didn't come out? You had your reasons, but now you're in a position you didn't want to be in. You wouldn't be in this situation had you stopped it in its tracks. The odd thing here is that it happens to the outgoing as much as it does the shy. Introverts and extroverts alike have their respective reasons for letting things like this slide and it's shameful the way we censor ourselves. I was tired of censoring myself physically and verbally. So, I said the hell with it. I'm going to learn to punch people in the face.

Self-defense would help any shmuck get the confidence to walk around with his/her head high in this ball-breaking world. (I hate having my [womanly] balls broken). Before finding the gym home I patronize now, I had joined a certain gym that similarly catered to MMA, Ju Jitsu, Boxing, and sideways kicking the shit out of stuff. I didn't bat an eye at the inflated price of this place (you get what you pay for). I wasn't intimidated when one of the instructors took us through "supersets" of these ab incinerating sit ups. I even I smiled in glee as we burnt ourselves out on punching bags until our left hooks felt like we were making contact with that big cinderblock those idiot novice karate students try to chop against the advisement of their sensei's. *Not yet, grasshopper, you are not ready.*

I invested in a personal trainer to tell me all the common sense health stuff I should already know and throw in some exercises for good measure. I used my B-Day and Christmas fund for this and was ready to change my life (ten pounds down later, my life was changed alright, but not just in the weight department).

Let's call my personal muscle mouth, Maxwell, a 36-year-old professional fighter from the south who accomplished a world of victories in the fitness realm despite never having left his back yard of a hometown. Who outside of trashy novels gets hit on by a trainer? Probably lots of girls. But who the hell does it take two weeks to get the hint? None other than this striking young muffin eater you see before you. I was so focused on not looking like a fool huffing and puffing trying to get my size twelve to a size eight that I didn't realize I had been entertaining the subtle advances of Maxwell. Once I figured it out however; I didn't take immediate action. Honestly it didn't bother me, and I did not take it seriously. What woman would mind a couple of compliments here or there from an MMA fighter/trainer that sees beautiful women all day long and judges her body a contender? What woman wouldn't want to believe that their huffing and sweating like a farm animal during a workout wasn't as off-putting as it felt? I ignored it and everything was fine, until that day we were sparring outside and things got a little heavy, and blatant.

"You know, I love those little noises you make when we work out. I'd like to hear them amplified if we could get some alone time together; Perhaps starting with a massage?" he asked as I punched at him and dodged. It was the third week. That was the first time he'd outwardly proposed something physical. I froze like a deer in headlights. Two seconds later I could feel my defense mechanism kicking in. I couldn't help it,

"What are you laughing at?" he asked surprised. I couldn't speak just yet, so I just kept punching, dodging and guffawing like an imbecile. Yes, I was shocked, and I had a nervous giggle. But for the love of God the pseudo smoothness with which he orchestrated these comments...it was unfair to ask me to not to laugh. His slightly squinted bedroom eyes paired with a crooked cocky grin and a little sexual shudder of his shoulders at the "perhaps a massage" part (which was said in a low-budget porno growl) was just too damn much. It sent me over the edge.

"So can I take that as a yes?" he asked helping me from the ground.

"I'm married." I reminded him. We left it at that, that day.

I was in a dilemma. I genuinely liked Maxwell as a trainer and a person. He was wise and driven when it came to health. He was funny enough to distract me from the pain, and he was never aggressive. On the other hand, I knew I needed to switch trainers. I absolutely HATED awkward situations. I didn't want to make trouble and have to start all over with someone new. Who would want to work with me after hearing I did away with their co-worker? It would only be a couple of weeks more. I figured I'd paid the money, I was getting results, and I could tough it out. WRONG. The end of the line happened towards the end of our time together. We had just done running drills and worked on boxing techniques. We stopped for wall-sits and he wanted my input on luxury hotels for an event he was putting together.

"Fancy." Was my response to almost all the pictures he'd scroll by. My thighs were starting to burn as I sat against the wall. To distract myself, I concentrated hard on the different images of Jacuzzis, full buffets, king sized beds, flat screen televisions, gourmet brunch menus, aaaand a penis...

In the frame-of-mind I was in, I stared trying to comprehend what I was seeing. I thought it was some kind of breakfast sausage a hotel was showing off as an example of one of the buffet items sans the side dish and parsley, but no. it was a thick, brown, uncircumcised penis. My thighs buckled, wobbling me to the concrete. This is what happens when you don't speak up.

"Maxwell!"

"What?" he smirked.

"Why?!" I asked. Shock had deleted my immediate vocabulary.

"I wanted you to understand what you were getting into." He said simply as he slid to the ground with me. I was at a loss for words,

"But I-I never...what do you mean by—"

"—shh, I understand. You're 'married' " he air-quoted. "You don't seem to have much experience with this, so I figured I'd give you a preview. To get you ready."

"I don't know what gave you the idea that I'm going to cheat on my husband with you." I insisted, creating more space between us.

"Well you're still here with me aren't you? Any uninterested woman would have fired me by now." Well he had a fucking point didn't he? To let him go had been my first instinct, but passivity said *NO, don't make waves, just tough it out, it's harmless.*

My passivity, which never proved to cause that much trouble for me before, was making me a bad wife.

I wanted to backtrack all the way to our first meeting so I could slap that unassuming smile off my face and send a blazing smoke signal exploding into the words "please do not try to seduce the betrothed introvert. She's too timid to tell you to fuck off!"

After that ordeal, I just wanted to forget it ever happened, and go home to have a big juicy ribeye steak and some chocolate buttercream topped cake. So much for my size eight. The moral here is that you can choose to be calm and go with the flow and get suckered into a bad situation, or you can learn to focus, and woman/man the hell up before you start sinking. There's literally quicksand everywhere, and no one can save you once you're shoulders deep.

Also, a quick side note, don't accept Sprite if you asked for Coke. Don't be an ass about it, but you deserve your Coke just like every other good tax paying citizen of this country. You've had a long day at work; you're going to have to stop and pump gas in the cold on the way home to your roommate's messy clutter. Send the damn Sprite back and get your Coke. Life is hard enough, isn't it?

> **Every time you don't speak up you send a micro-message of inadequacy to yourself.**

I wanted to emphasize the importance of speaking up even in the smaller situations like the Sprite because every time you don't speak up you send a micro-message of inadequacy to yourself. You might as well be saying "I'm not worth the extra time it would take to get what I asked for in the first place." Other people certainly don't hesitate to make us feel this way. Why would we inject ourselves with this lie of not being capable of saying: *"no, not that one!"*

Volcanoes

Some of us were volcanoes in a past life
Could've been something else
But had a mission way too hot to be anything human
Women were once fire mountains
We were sulfuric geysers ready to sing and meet the
sky Somewhere in between
We were colors...the blue of the sea
Reflective in all its raw light and aquatic fury
We used to populate in water births
And give life to evolution
We were revolutions
Wars for change
And city rains
Before there were cities
Our spirits turned the stomachs of gods proclaiming
woe to flawed creations
We were creators
The mediums between darkness and life
What is more powerful than a womb
What other matriarchal symbol can hold so many
birthdays?

We were the caves and curves of Africa in her thriving
state
When pyramids played sundial with the sky
And the moon lived two doors down from heaven
WE WERE mothers of the cosmos. Taught the universe
how to speak to God and taught the wind to love
herself after she taught us how to fly
Why...have we traded our wings in exchange for
insecurities?

Why are we on bended knees
Prostrate before men and trees, trying to find love in
idolatry?
Sisters of the human race seem to share the strange
desire
To worship the pain, lust, greed
And follow demons into the fire
We are dying. Spiritually.
We are Leaves dancing and spitting ashes from the
same burning Tree.
In threesomes with materialism, sex, and society,
Mistaking these for the holy Trinity

I miss the long walks I would take in the Garden
Adam, God and I
In Eden
Before the fruit called me out of my womanhood

Tricked me out of
my right to be pure
and a human star
I was once able to
move mountains
with my faith
At one time I could
hold whole
conversations with
the night sky
I could scold the
sea for his many
mistresses
And I knew the
secrets the sun hid

behind his back
But I have forgotten
I was a palm tree, I was baptismal rainfall from storm
I was a sun shower
I was a warrior
I was a princess
I WAS A QUEEN
I knew I was beautiful
I ruled with my spirit and cast evil from my part of the
Earth
I dreamt I was volcano in a past life
Could've been something else but had a mission way
too hot to be anything human
Our mission is too hot to be anything less than
phenomenal women
A firestorm of SHE.

The Broken Promise Land

Held captive on the broken promise land
Barefoot and broken back
Looking up into the beaming eyes of the heat hot sun
for mercy

Was God listening?
Could he
See the tears that watered the rice plants and
Washed the rough hands of our African ancestry
My memory is festering as I recall before
My generation was born
The systematic destruction of our race
So that we could stand where we are today
See blacks beaten blue
My paper bleeds for my great grandmothers
Broken grandfathers
America was a dying forest of Ethiopian wood
Our daughters and sons...too many of our native sons
have set
Into graves before their time

I hear they used to execute people like me
Even the people like me who were tending to their own
Were taken behind some abandoned farm were
Promised a slow, savory death lashed against skin
were
Forced to run seeking salvation in the dark
Trying to follow the drinking gourd
Fields of us death-dancing in air
Some of our brothers and sisters still hang there

I'm sick of seeing history repeat himself
Queens wear shackles of promiscuity
And find salvation in being whipped into submission
by today's rappers
Chains shine like daylight hugging necks of young
princes like silver nooses
We still hang there
History's timeless scaffold
Our bruises still be visible
These black skin-deep wounds still hurt when touched
Massa's chains, now rusted beneath brown skin, are
brittle enough to break
But we still carry them in the flesh of our wrists and
ankles
Like memories too thick to fade

Memories,
think back before the nightmares
Of lashes falling like rain upon bodies too worn to
stand
Think back
Before our Royal melanin was reduced to the color of
dirt
When the native sons arose too infinite to set
Or be weighed down by metal
In pharaohs time
When a Queens's glory was measured by the beads of
her robe
Rather than the shortness of her skirt.

Princes were raised to become kings
We constructed pyramids with work ethic and will

What happened?
Brothers and sisters take your place
Won't you help sing these redemption songs?
Can you taste the melody?
The spirit of enslaved tongues singing this generation
Awake and into the arms of emancipation?
"Emancipate yourselves from mental slavery
None but ourselves can free our minds."
 Marley, Truth, King, Tubman, Mandela, Malcolm,
Marshall, Sanchez, Giovanni, Obama
Our prophets
Leave footprints

"Will we march on till victory is won?"
Or will the legacy end here?

CHAPTER 5: CAPTURE

The fifth step in your Monster hunt is to capture the thing! No one was around to see you slay your own beast that stood 9 feet higher than you with its fangs, and claws. It's okay; you were secure enough not to need a witness to your drama. It was a messy encounter, and you are covered in monster blood, but think of it as a transfusion. That's the blood your inner monster had been sucking from you for years! You got your life source back, and now you've captured it. It's quite lonely in that cage you put the monster in. You know what it's like to feel lonely, but you better not start showing mercy now. You've got water to boil. You have got to start cutting up the veggies and start choosing seasonings.

"Peeling Off the Layers of Lonely"

Did you enjoy your own company before being told you need to get out more? Are other people's perceptions of loners the cause of your feelings of loneliness? Some people are positively afraid of being on their own; others find it boring/pathetic, and there are just those who are addicted to the company of a crowd. Sadly, that mentality is contagious.

I had an aggressive case of the diabetic "lonelies" as a preteen. Like an overdrawn pancreas that ran out of insulin, my inner light stopped shining. I became desperate for friendships, however superficial, however fake...I just needed people who would get people to stop looking at me like I was broken. I needed my social insulin.

I needed people at my middle school to see me like they saw themselves. To see me as a functional human being and not just some weird, shy girl. I suppose I got what I asked for when I met "them."

"So rule number one stop walking so stiff and standing around like you're scared. You scared?" a mouthy 8th grader Tazzy said as she suddenly bucked and I jumped,

"No," I replied, only slightly lying.

"Good. Rule two, you're cute, but you got a mustache, cut that shit or Malik will never talk to you. Get your mom to take you to the spa. Oh, and wear this," she tossed me a lip gloss and taunted, "Don't you have anything tighter? Your shirt loose as hell; yall look at her shirt!"

I was surrounded by five giggling girls from the cool crowd whom I wasn't sure if I liked or not. The ringleader who was speaking, Tazzy, was giving me the overview of how people saw me and how I could change it. When I was going to pull out my notepad so I could take notes, Debbie slapped my hand.

"That right there is why they all call you a nerdy-assed loser," Debbie said.

"They say that?" I asked, refusing to let the tears come.

"Yeah girl, you always have your nose in a book writin' and stuff. What is there to write about? And the only thing more boring than a book is more than one book. You got like 6 of them on you every day! Nerdy-ass." Debbie said, filing away her nails along with the membrane of my soul. I'd reasoned to find something high to jump from when I got home.

"They won't say that for long." Tazzy was behind me doing something to my hair, "Malik didn't say that. And if you stick with us, he won't."

Malik was perfect. I puppy loved Malik like a rabid poodle in a fur coat. I could see him from where we were sitting. And asked,

"So how do I get people to notice me?"

Have you ever lost yourself in a gratifying Purgatory? This is the place between getting what you want and trying to hold on to things in life that matter more than your desires. You may have finally been inducted into some secret society that you've been obsessed with for seven years, but they tell you that you must never speak to your family again. Maybe you become famous and get to hang out with the ladies from The View, but your schedule doesn't allow time for your spouse/significant other. Purgatory is a half lit Hell with no fire.

Why is it that we are so willingly succumb to change the minute there's pressure to do so? Why the hell does the way we live our lives have to fit the majority's ruling of what is "normal." It takes damaged relationships, decisions that can't be undone, and looking in the mirror at an outright stranger before we understand that the aliens have probed us into submission, and we are carbon copies of a group of people who couldn't care less for us. What for? For acceptance. Is it ever worth it?

When loneliness appears to be the only thing your brain remembers about your life; survive it. Avoid feeding into the myth that groups are the only way to travel, and have a bagel by yourself unapologetically sometime. Act like you like yourself.

Don't make this a source for depression or pain. Save the pain for that monster inside trying to destroy you by backing you into a corner, and putting you into an illusion of a lonely cage. No, you turn around right now and put that thing in a cage, then set it on fire.

Silence

She tongue kisses silence like the man that won't let her go.
He stalks her shadow deep.
Silence is obsessed with his girl.
He likes to sleep in her esophagus and wake up on the roof of her mouth screaming his quiet through her breath.
A seed in her throat that won't be swallowed before it sprouts.

Solitaire

I have discovered God
The earth
quakes under the footsteps of his early return
to his children
I have discovered me
Human
Heir to the afterlife...but tied under earthly anarchy
Evolution marks us archaic....we are ageless.

I have discovered us
God and I
God. Is. Love.
I am carved in his image,
So aren't I
Love?

Why am I looking for it?

Why would I ever prowl through the streets quiet and
stalking for another half
When I was born to complete the circumference of
myself?
I have no control
Over the beauty in the disfigured math where one and
one create **one**
Add em'
Two complete individuals becoming **one**
Eve and Adam
Even on a nuclear level, two mere halves would lead to
explosion

Atoms
We must learn to punctuate our own sentences before
we cursive write Novellas
Across our papyrus hearts
Across the sky in cloud ink
Across gardens while dotting our I's with poppy seeds
My heart is a just an old rag used to shine the most
beautiful Golden statues,
Priceless gems and trophies
But I am still a King

Chiseled from the marrow of the universes spine,
Descendant of stardust
I was dust
born into royalty
Deemed ruler of my fate
But in my faith
I still ache under my confusion
And the notion I am incomplete
needing to search
For another half
They tell me I should be looking to harvest my
happiness from someone else's laugh
But I am no thief
I know joy
I found it in the back of my throat hiding between
voice and Thought
I found it on the inside of a prayer
I found it in this crown I once hid
I found it in the poems I spit
I found it in the riddles I talk, and the fact that my
sentences never come out quite right

I found it last night in the beauty of my flaws
I found it after my last break up
I found it in the mouth of my most recent first kiss
I found it in the aftermath of an implosion
I found it alone and
Complacent in solitude
Playing solitaire ensures you won't lose what you came
in with
Why gamble?
Instead, learn to play alone

I'll deal three in my Eden tree
Happy up here with close friends and novels
One day
He'll sit next to me in this garden
Fashioned from heavens hands and sands from
Genesis
He will come bearing no gifts
And will not speak the language of the others
He will be dressed modestly
And ask me for nothing but company

That's when I'll say
I'd like you to come break something with me
Let's tear social conventions and burn them with fire
we borrow From Venus
Let's swing from chandeliers and create glass rains
That shatter into splashes of diamonds
Let's sing
Memories of our future and forget the physics of time
Come to the kingdom and let me shine
Your completeness with mine

Your heart is full and now needs a throne room
You may oblige my chest

Praise the body and the heartbeat
The human mind, the hands and the spine
Don't you know we built like pyramids
Ancient and ageless
Architecture and art
With the promise of death somewhere hidden inside
I AM afraid, I AM honest, I AM ugly
I AM fire, I AM beautiful, I AM human
So I have found it
My reflection
I have discovered God
I see him through the mirror's brown eyes
So there is love
There is me
And I refuse to search

CHAPTER 6: COOK

Imagine yourself a chef! You ARE Bobby Flay, and your show is about to begin. The smell of the broth is hypnotic.

1c garlic salt
2c lemon juice
2 Handfuls of chili powder, pepper, onion powder, and cumin
3 bay leaves
46 drops of licorice root

The monster is pleading for you to reconsider, but you're not about to waste this delicious smelling broth are you? You've put the vegetables in and it's time to COOK your inner monster.

Cookery is a pretty prevalent theme in Dante's descent thru the nine circles of his Hell, and just imagine the smell of melting Demons! Your monster is much fresher. I promise you it will smell 16 times better. Careful about lowering his cage down into the soup, you may want to put in your ear plugs because it will holler out all the screams you've ever internally screamed from whatever pain it was causing you. Reassure your monster that this will hurt him more than it will hurt you. For once.

"Make Believe: More Than Mere Child's Play"

I've got an imaginary friend. This is something I advocate. I could tell you that I actually think someone is here, with me, every second of every day and night, or I could make it simpler and tell you that our imaginary friends are extensions of ourselves that help us shut up and deal...with struggle, with agony, with loss, with life. Tristan, my imaginary friend, is a part of me I have projected onto my physical space in order to better handle the unexpected things that might sway me to go binge eating, drinking or doing something weird like hammering my thumbs to feel alive. Tristan suggests painting. He's a fan of yoga, long hot bubble baths, and calming the hell down before I give myself a heart attack.

He was there during all eight teeth I've had pulled as a kid, the night before I got on an airplane for the first time, and that time I almost got pushed into that back room with that handsy server at that restaurant (together we ducked beneath his meaty arm and ran). Tristan was often there when people on the physical plane weren't. He was there when college got to be too much, and I hadn't had sleep in close to three days. I was offered a "pick-me-up", and I spent the better half of two days plastered to the shower wall convinced that my exes were coming to kill me and that the police would find out I took something and take me in for two life sentences.

Tristan helped me laugh at myself instead of crying over the exam that I still ended up bombing after all that. Tristan sitting on the edge of my bed was the only way I could get to sleep that night. If my referring to an imaginary presence by name is making you uncomfortable, from here on out replace the concept of "Tristan" with how you visualize your inner strength.

What about your circumstance has driven you to question your worth, capability, or potential? How in the world has something beyond your control put you in a position to look at yourself negatively? Learning to play up the internal positives in the face of physical negatives keeps the soul unclogged and able to take care of you through even your most screwed up periods in life.

I've learned not to measure my worth within the metric system of my circumstances. I was once in an emotionally abusive relationship as an underclassman in high school where all my negatives were constantly being shoved at me. In the day time, I would frolic in the dead flowers that grew out of his mouth into insults. Shouting matches degenerated into silence between us. Late at night when I couldn't find sleep behind my cried-out puffy eyelids, Tristan and I watched "Three's Company," and read Archie comics. On date nights with this person, despite my walking on eggshells, the evening always ended the same, "Stupid, what the hell did you say that for?" "God damn you're dumb, I can't even finish this conversation right now." "Just shut the fuck up." Eventually, Tristan began sticking around whenever I saw this person so I could manage to keep the damn buckets of tears dry inside my face. I was so thankful when this other girl caught his attention. I picked up and ran as fast as I could.

I literally ran. As a new hobby. Getting some extra cardio in, I made up games to stop the lactic acid build up in my legs from making me want to steal someone's wheelchair. I'd pretend I was being chased by zombies. God, the zombies smelled awful; like rotten meat and used sponges. Friends I'd try to get to do this with me thought it was weird, but those were the same people not burning off those stress hormones, and that

> **Pretend you're being chased by Death and ironically, you'll live longer.**

Popeye's grease from lunch. Think about it, pretend you're being chased by Death, and ironically, you'll live longer. Make believe makes life more productive than being stuck in reality.

My father once pretended he'd been kidnapped by some local terror group to cover up a three-day disappearance while my mother was pregnant with me. With a shaved head, ripped clothes, and eyes that seem to have seen down the back of Satan's throat he told his abduction story to the family and the police who filed an official report. No one knew this was false until YEARS later.

THAT'S the kind of commitment I'm talking about (obviously replacing the fat ass lie with your own constructive make believe that will make your life easier). Commit like you've got some shit to lose, and don't allow yourself to feel ashamed of pretending your call center day job is Mission Control and you've got to bring those damn rockets back down to earth in the next two minutes, or we're all going down! Aaaaand scene.

Even the bosses at our jobs play pretend. My very first boss hated me down to my 14-year-old guts. He and his wife were friends of the family that owned a hair store. His wife was my mother's best friend, so he was pretty much forced into letting me work there. Granted, I was a pretty horrible employee. I had crippling social phobia around this time, so yeah, I couldn't actually *talk* to the customers. I'm being generous. I avoided the customers like the plague, and I felt sick every time someone new came in the door. I also had a thing with stress eating back then, so when we were slow, but I was anticipating the Saturday rush, I ate six Twix bars in one sitting like a damn goat. All this guy saw me do was eat and stock merchandise (the wrong way most of the time). He'd smile and not say much to me, gritting his teeth as he let the twenty-five dollars fall into my hands at the end of the day.

Looking closer, I knew that smile had been a grimace all along. Pretending helped us both get through that summer

I needed job experience, and he needed not to have to sleep on the couch because of an angry wife. I understood the truth to be completely predictable. Upon visiting my hometown, I found he'd been bringing my name up, less than reputably, in conversations having to do with ne'er-do-wells, slackers, and people most likely to fail at life. Just talking shit.

But AGAIN, pretending helped us both get through that summer. The goal was met through the elements of make-believe. You don't always have to be okay with your situation, but you *will* always have to deal with it. Why not build up your imagination in the process?

Pretending helps preserve your personality as you know it. Pretending chases away the bitterness you could feed into, the pettiness you could exhibit, and serves as a safety rope as you fall into life's little bottomless pits. It's not being fake, it is survival. Vincent Phipps, my mentor, used to tell me that closing your eyes relaxes your brain by 20 percent. And if you close your eyes and visualize yourself doing better with whatever you're up to at the moment, you'll raise the likelihood of a successful outcome. Playing pretend as an adult is just advanced visualization. Why stop at deep breathing? Close your damn eyes and go to Panama with that cute sale associate you've been eyeing at Walmart every Tuesday. After that, open them back up, grab your imaginary friend and take in a matinee. A large popcorn will be half off. Eat the whole freaking thing yourself. You deserve it.

On Night's Like These I Listen to Banks Music

And I drove me crazy. And I drove me crazy. **And I drove me crazy.**

And I drove me crazy. And I drove me crazy.

And I drove me crazy.

And I drove me crazy.

And I drove me crazy.   AND. I. DROVE.
ME. CRAZY.

And I drove me crazy.

And I drove me crazy.

And I drove me crazy. **And I drove me crazy.**

And I drove me crazy.

And I drove me crazy.   And I drove
me crazy.

And I drove me crazy.   And I drove
me crazy.

AND I DROVE ME CRAZY. AND I DROVE ME CRAZY.

And I drove me crazy. And I drove me crazy.

And I drove me crazy.

CHAPTER 7: SAY YOUR GRACE

You can't break bread or bone without thanking the heavens you've made it this far. Wow. It's time to plate and serve. You've cooked your inner beast to a pulp. People have told you to pray your demons away. People have told you that evil has a plan for you just as well as good does, and you have to decide who your master will be. People have told you to face the ugly in you, and look at what you've done! You've taken steps to pulverize it. This monster, in particular, is under your control. This is not to say that this is the last time you will use your cauldron sized stock pot. For your first time, however; you've got to give thanks that you stuck with it!

God's Glass Ceilings

I've always seen the face of my Creator as a grandmother. An older, wiser woman who gave birth to most of the room. I have to choose my own switch to get whipped with when I challenge karma, and she is always on my side when she knows I am trying.

Someone once told me that the more intelligent you are, the less religious you become. I was 19, Baptist, and mildly offended by this comment. Now 300 years and a world of spiritual evolutions later I've broken down this statement and have found myself agreeing with it.

I used to take the word "religious" to mean belief in God. But let's consider how loosely this word is used. When people engage in habitual behavior, we say they are doing a thing "religiously." Someone attends church or Bible study; we think them religious even though we know nothing of their personal struggles with life, relationship with a deity, or behavior. Any person who puts the rituals/habits of a faith into practice could be called religious. This is to say that one can be "religious" without taking to heart a belief in any deity. There are several reasons one might just go through the motions of a religion: vying for a spot in a pleasant afterlife, peace of mind in this chaotic world, family expectations, or to find a friend/spouse to name a few. That is not deep enough to speak to where a person's spirit is or what it is capable of.

Seeing this large divide between belief and ritualism in the definition of religion made my friend's statement clearer to me. It is a statement that can speak to the difference between a thinker and a blind believer. Neither is better than the other. They have opposing spiritual needs. For the sake of perspective, I will use the Christian faith to frame the differences.

The thinker is the Christian who, through some means, has formed a foundation for their belief in God and keeps it healthy through a combination of asking the tough questions, careful philosophical thought, talking to people of other faiths, reading articles, and persevering in their pursuit of a better understanding of the human condition. There are variations of thinkers. Some never get past the stage of the tough questions or perhaps are having a hard time balancing their article reading and philosophical thought with taking care of kids or going to work. None of that matters because a thinker will always be a thinker even if all they have time for is to thank their God for another day of life and sun.

A thinker will always wonder of the larger concepts and will never be truly content or satiated in going through the motions. Thus the thinker is the less "religious" because to the thinker, ritualism is a mystery that they are intensely curious about. In the case of Christianity, what is this about the concept of Sin, bone, blood, and communion? What is it in those moments when we are rebirthed by water during baptism that creates a miracle even now in the 21st century? Is prophecy an inside joke that time has with fate? Is humanity the butt of that joke?

Despite the opinion of some blind believers, the goal of the thinker is not to end up in the silent embrace of shadowed corners, webbed in grief asking "what is the meaning of life! What is it?!" rocking in fetal position. The Thinker does not wish to find definite answers, but to open their minds, conceptualize, discuss, and understand. There you have it, "The more intelligent you are, the less religious you become" because your spirit has outgrown the dogma of "I must do to believe" and insists on spiritual exploration.

The blind believer is the one who thinks less and convicts more. The blind believer will value the conviction, regular church/function attendance, and the converting of non-Christians more than he will value the growth of his own mind and spirit. He is not unintelligent, but he is not as willing to expand and think about ideas that he feels aren't rooted somewhere in scripture or in the words of his pastor, evangelist, minister, or fellow disciples. These are the people you find who have the kind of faith that will allow them to stand in the metaphorical "fire" and put all their trust in the hands of their God even in the ugliest of circumstances. They walk by faith, not by sight.

Herein lies the struggle and difference between the two. One does not need to ask and discuss. The other draws his faith from an unending well of larger ideas about humanity/souls. What if a portion of people who identify themselves as agnostic or a type of atheist were grand level thinkers trying to force themselves into a blind believer paradigm? Some of us must think and examine to build faith. If those around us discourage that kind of faith, what are we left with but the need to isolate ourselves from the white walls and locked doors?

The universe has no floors or ceilings. It is an endless hallway with doors, stairs, and shelves. Blind believers don't make a habit of leaving their rooms. Thinkers cannot be contained, and therefore many thinkers may fall away thinking that containment is the only way to prove their faith, and therefore they lose faith in faith.

Protect your spirit, watch out for cults, and know your belief is as much yours as your own blood. Don't take anyone else's just because you are nudged to do so. Read. Understand. Learn. Quiet your mind, and decide. You are human, therefore limitless and inherently spiritual.

Earth's Little Hell

I lost a lot of blood
I mean you know, with the broken stained glass and
all
Nothing but colorful lies anyway
The whole cathedral was fake
After the ice sculptures melted
And all the candles went out you'd think
We would've been suspicious
But we were distracted by the night

The darkness took delight in itself
And swelled with the hot noise of
Pious silence
The quiet can fill up space just as good as gravity can
when given a chance
We gave it a chance, all of us in the cult.
Did chants, succumbed to trance
And carried the bulk
Of conviction on our sinful shoulders
But that wasn't enough to get away from the flames
The cruel game of extremism held those hot coals over
our heads
Forced us to bow
Dared us to ask why
Tipped around stapling guilt to our spines

And the leader came
Tall blind and intimidating
Said "hating is not the way, judging's bad too

But hand out these leaflets or woe be to you."

Most records of my history were kept in dried up tears,
lies, incomplete documents, and burnt up pictures. I
was born culturally Lost,
Spiritually disadvantaged, and historically ignorant.
My past is hard to get to
Because earth never spun in my people's direction.
And you think I'll find my soul in leaflets
Written by the people that indoctrinated my people to
keep this
Cycle of oppression in generational rotation?

Pass down to the next
Pass down to the next

"Your mission is submission"
I said getting up from my knees
Please do not insult my freedoms further by asking me
to sit down.
No, I've been down too long
It's time I rose up, rose a fist
Adopted these roses that grow from the concrete in my
mind
And become unashamed
Of this hunger for
Liberation. Knowledge. FREEDOM
God is freedom, soul is freedom, flesh is freedom,
knowing where You came from and loving it is
freedom, science is freedom Practicing religion is
freedom...
It's the guilt that puts you in jail. The cultish mentality
is the Earths little Hell

Satan's Hymn

I'm going to sink your spirit deep
I'm going to whisper to you in your sleep
I'm gonna make you feel alone
I'm gonna make you feel so low
So so low...

You may want to string yourself up somewhere high
By the time I'm finished with you.
Like a puppet slaved to its strings or the skeletal
carcass of a Human
Hanging from a tree.
Dance for me.
Feel the heat licking your feet like you're standing on a
beach
Where lava's in the sea.
Jump in.

I've wanted you since you were born.

You're just a soul with a body
Crippled and can't fly.
Paste your shame to your spine,
And let me massage you
I'll tell you why you're not strong enough to resist flesh
You looked so good in that little black dress
Last night...and the morning after.
I'd swear you were mine.

You had eyes like a gypsy jeweled over with plastic
lashes
Thighs that lived for music

So hot, you were sweating ashes
And I know you heard me calling to you!
I was cat calling to you.
I was standing on the wall, I was passing you another bottle,
I pulled your hair and snapped your back forward.
I figured the closer your face is to the ground
The more at home you'd feel;
The closer to me you'd feel
And when you make that long walk home, alone,
Freshly fermented;
And your insides are still burning liquid
I'm going to watch your crown and jewels all fall into the toilet
Cascading like a digested waterfall.
Splashing like drunken firebombs made of rhinestones and plastic Silver
Mistakes oozing out of the mouth of a pseudo good girl
Who thought she was above falling for my tricks.

It's fun to watch the Earth fall from the shoulders of a queen
It makes her ass all the more rounder.
And you know thick girls have the all the fun at my parties.
Oh, what you crying? That's fine...I like my women broken.
Oh, what you praying? Okay, cool. I'll be waiting for you when You're done
Prayers always go unheard.
Your human words smell too much like you've been talking to me.

Be real, there are better things you could be doing on
your knees
Don't waste your time fallen Queen.
You are a captive now
Come with me.

Speak the language of lies let your spirit fall asleep
Bound by my chains, I'll set you free.
How supreme
You'll feel wading in the fiery streams.
Mistaking Ménage à trois for the Trinity
Ain't no woman ever been a volcano
Fuck your empowerment, I'll devour you.
You. so guilty. So desirous.
So shameful. So self-centered.
Forgiveness? What is that?
Come with me into this twisted fantasy.
I won't bite
Fall to the earth drink in the world's raw light
Let me love you red and black like a massacre at night.

CHAPTER 8: FEED

SOUP'S ON! It's time for the best part. The main event! This is your feast. You could invite friends I suppose, but I can't guarantee they will be able to stomach the shit you went thru that created this monster in the first place, and you don't want to make your friends ill. It's best you make this a table for one and put this thing to a digestive rest in peace. You created it, you cooked it, you are the one that should feed. Screw calories just for the moment. This is good eatin', and you WILL gain a few.

"Fruit, Labor, and GAINZ!"

I observe fitness as some would the institution of religion. Let's use Christianity as a framework again. The spiritual experience of understanding your body through a litany of fitness wisdom can be pieced together seamlessly. After tucking and rolling out of the situation with Maxwell the muscle mouth, I found my new gym home. To continue to have faith in the process of becoming fit and strong, I needed to train different and hold myself accountable for learning how to take care of my temple. It's not just the gym that makes the difference, similar to how a specific church isn't going to be the difference between salvation and death.

A good worship facility, with Bible-based values, equates to a good fitness facility with goals and education for its members. Both are fertile places to begin sowing your seeds and bearing fruit of your labors. Carrying on a healthy spiritual life and keeping a strong relationship with Christ is a labor of love for Christians; it's hard work with many of the rewards only coming from one's faith. It is a relationship that values faith over sight. You have to have faith in your body to submit and change underneath your improved habits even if you don't see those changes right away. If you stop, you will NEVER see them. There is no overnight, perfect body/health just like there are no insta-Christians. Both of these journeys require failure in order to be renewed. They require constant practice and effort to get better.

The pendulum of Sin and Repentance is a common theme that stitches the fundamentals of fitness and religion together. If you are a person of faith (any faith) you know your mission, your goals, and what is or isn't permissible by the deity/doctrine of your religion. But how many times have you found yourself breaking those convictions? The Spirit was willing, but the flesh was weak and in the face of temptation you failed your test. In the fitness world, this is "hitting your limit." For example, when you max out on how many times you can lift that dumbbell before you are tempted to put it down.

You know you've got just one more in you, the mind is willing, but the flesh is weak, and you drop it. Sometimes hitting the limit simply means going to a company party and eating five doughnuts when you know good and well you'd already eaten. You weren't mentally well prepped enough to deny yourself that weakness yet, so doughnuts were your limit. When you can fight through that repeatedly, and when you finally say NO to the doughnuts after saying yes every time you saw them, you inevitably get stronger. Keep hitting your limit and eventually, you become limitless.

In fitness, conviction gives the journey structure. If you are Christian, perhaps your convictions consist of meeting with your weekly life groups, beginning your day with a prayer of thanks, sharing your faith with three people a week, and not having sex before marriage. Convictions keep us on track and motivate us to do better with our journey. Without convictions, there's no accountability. There is no growth. There is no sacrifice for what you believe in.

Education is vital to any journey. Being convicted to do the wrong things because of misinformation will have us all fat, sick, and upset when it comes to fitness.

Christians study the Bible, but with fitness, the information could come from all sorts of places. It is vital to have successful people in your life to filter out the garbage. This will help to avoid taking weird pills and going on cayenne pepper, lemon juice, and potato skin diets that claim overnight success. (Just like ordering a televangelist's "Holy Water" in order to find insta-Jesus...it just doesn't work that way). Surround yourself with the folks you want to look like. Eat with them, lift with them, dance with them, and stop canceling on them when they invite you to come running!

These journeys both require community. How can you expect to stick to your journey all by yourself, or worse, around people on an opposite path than you?

You hang with pizza eaters often enough, and you will have a slice. You hang out with people that eat protein and veggies every three hours; maybe they'll share with you and give you tips. See yourself as the creator and your body as your clay. Does the creator seek to serve us or do we live at the mercy of him/her? Think about that the next time your body (the creation) is demanding things like crispy Shrimp with garlic butter and a side of fries from you (the creator).

Do what is best for your creation and break it down. You are in charge, not your body. Sanctify your temple so it will learn discipline, temperance, and it will be trained to have some good sense at a buffet table.

Who is Body?

2 eyebrows
Face
Lips, hair, knees
Waist.
Body wants to be seen
Body wants appreciation and caress,
to rest and to live
Body works hard for life
Breathes and heaves exhales
Cells fight in white and red
Blood covers the tissue walls
And down the hall pumps the Mecca
Body worships heart, lung, and mind
Spine is a yogi that hums hymns of peace and
standing.
Bending. Landing.
Dancing. Sitting lotus
Body's focus is you.

You are the only consciousness body has ever known
The only spirit to own
His bones and skin
Body wants to be loved
And doesn't understand why you make her fly on a
synthetic high when she is sick
So quick to get lit off cough syrup and pills pills pills to
soothe her ills
Body wants to eat a rainbow
To see his pains flow away and under his plate

Even when body is on a date, she doesn't want a steak

He's got enough blood and enough marrow
Tomorrow body will ask you to stop
Constant bathroom stops after taco bell
Body is trying to reason with you,

You piece of God brain-child.

Try to remember what the earth is for
Its seeds and crops and water's more
Important than crave and eat
Sleep and eat
White or wheat
Spinach or meat
Strong or weak?
You decide.

"Feed me."
Body prays to you
May your answer come from light and
And inspiration from the hills
May you reassure body that she is a sensational beast
That she deserves better than what she thinks she
needs
Tell her she is a manifestation of the only things the
Earth knows about love

Tell body his heartbeat carries the rhythm of this
planet and that he shares a soul with the mountain
tops
Iced over on harsh days, but an insurmountable
summit, superior
Submitting itself before nothing

And that the atmosphere is rigged, fixed up in her
favor
Human, you are on fire
You are the reason
You are what was before, and what will be long after
You are a poem to the universe
A work of unspeakable beauty

A Modest Proposal

I like to eat like a rainbow
Carrots, cheese, peas,
Arms, liver, heart...knees
I just wanna be healthy.
And fit
2016 and people still have you thinking
Drinking tonic and supplemental pills
Will hit
That goal
I know the taste of salivating over American food
The body of a slice of pizza in all its glorious
Triangular absolution
Is the only lover I have ever savored like a mantra on
my tongue
When I say that my stomach is a cemetery
I mean that I've swallowed down the hope of wiping
clean the Carbonated, hydrogenated bags dated
For 20 years from now
Preservative dope that goes down my throat
I mean that addiction isn't just about needle and vein
And back Alleys,
And Hollywood
It's burger chains,
Companies chain you to the back of that grease Vat
And tell you to open wide
Addiction is sugar and salt and
My stomach eulogizes this flavor
My trainer eats like a rainbow
Her body is a DaVinci diagram
Circulation runs like a New York subway system

And her veins; convex rivers at full bulge
She sweats levels of the food pyramid
Smells like prime rib stuffed with a perfectly balanced
medley
Of everything Eden grew
Her internal garden flushes health thru the whites of
her eyes
So when she tells me
I must
Then I do
She tells me I can't have fruit tomorrow....why?
I've got to be meticulous about sugar and carbs and
water and Fasted cardio
But not too much cardio
Calorie counting food scale
Don't eat after midnight
Get in six meals per day
Buy sweet potatoes in bulk
And dive head first
Into a chicken breast
Like a sex craved rooster in a cage
I propose a change
If we...the fitness degenerates of America
Gave up the fight
And found an alternative...
If we let the souls from the junk food graveyard go
And eat the flesh from another whose internal gardens
grow
We could absorb nutrition from that perfect blood and
bone
We could eat like rainbows
Her clothes cling to all that nutritious muscle tissue

Tissue that would marry mine and paint me a portrait of
Gain and strength
If I ate my trainer...
Her essence would supplement the hardship of
counting, Portioning, and contorting these damn
cravings I keep having into castles of conviction I
cannot escape from
I would start with her tongue
Having it inside my body will help me understand how
a person could taste the tit of an unbreaded chicken
and keep eating it in the name of health
Every day the heart creates enough energy to drive a
truck 20 Miles
I'd swallow hers whole
Making my gut a home for independent
Electronic impulse
I'll rotisserie her until her honey glaze and shine
Is a thing of dark, unimaginable health conscious
satisfaction
I'll fashion
My cravings for the hunt of healthy human flesh
Fitness made as easy as one mindful meal
Friends, do not be afraid to utilize the people you know
The ones with the tight skin and hard muscle
The ones with goldmines in their mouths
Talking about the arithmetic of acceptable eating
Take them to your homes
Let them feed you in ways other than food for thought
Fill yourselves with exactly what they have eaten.

The Female Body.

Strange how People always are begging to see it, touch
it, use it, talk about it...
But as soon as it's accessible, someone's a whore.
Someone is being dehumanized and ostracized for
giving into the pressure.
The female body is something so beautiful
It's dangerous, "sinful" and feared as much as it is
desired.
Then the females that give it, no questions asked,
and no money required
are grossly insulted by the same men who indulge in
their public service.
What in the actual fuck?

---the neighborhood virgin

CHAPTER 9

Now that you've conquered something that tried to defeat you, you should be hungry. Your new appetite calls you to identify the many monsters inside that you've still got to maul. Life assures new malicious creatures will appear regularly. As long as you are prepared, courageous, and hungry the more monsters, the merrier. Develop a craving for improvement while controlling your craving to create more bad stuff. As humans, that's what we're best at. Cravings.

"Consumption"

The word "Consumption" has a connotation that alludes to overindulgence or disease. These addictions and fixations eat us from the inside out until there is only a bit of fat and dried blood left caked to our bones. They drown us in our own monsters and dare us to come up for air. This chapter is a prelude to Volume 2 of *Monsters: Poetry on How to Bite Back*. It is a story involving: three characters, an addiction, a turtle, some good music, love, hate, a robot, a DJ, a possible ghost, a small house fire, two "petty poems" and a stick figure named Sam. I'm not going to ruin it for you, but this is serious business. I mean someone gets all up in the face of the person you love and tries to take what's yours what do you do?

A. Slap the donkey teeth out of their mouth
B. Take your love hostage
C. Put on your aluminum foil hat and ride the time machine back to the day you and your love were undisturbed
D. Cry into a pillow

Answer: Obviously take the hostage...

Just kidding!

You may have chosen donkey teeth... That is not ideal, nor is taking a hostage (trust me, too much duct tape involved). Those are poor choices unless you've taken out a loan for bail money already. Stop. Think. What does it mean to man/woman up? What will it take to summon the confidence to say, "What is mine will always be mine. What is not mine is none of my business."

Infatuation and addiction are the same shade of black, and Volume 2 is the literary illumination of the beauty of darkness. You've had your dinner and dose of self-help, now I will attempt to touch you like I know you. I want to crawl into bed with you, eat your food, become the you that you were as you were breaking under the weight of your infatuation.

Raz, Ade,' and the speaker of these poems are navigating a strange universe. I'm giving you a small taste of their all-consuming story told in poetry.

RAZ

"on waking, your mouth
come from your dream,
gave me the taste of earth,
of sea water, of seaweed,
of the depths of your life,
and I received your kiss
moistened by the dawn
as if it came to me next to the sea."

PABLO NERUDA

Waiting on Forever

How does it find us? Love.
It wasn't there before, but now it wants and bites and begs,
shivers out of the rafters
clogs up the toilet. All the while singing like the ghost it is,
the human it wants to be.
The chemistry between us was a gentle revolution.
Soft as the moment before you pull the trigger,
I couldn't see past you for years
DJ of my pulse, what did you do to me?
The premonitions of our future shook me from my sleep
Ruler of my spine, what did you do to me?
And so the nights went peacefully unslept
Devil on my angel's shoulder what did you do to me?
There were turntables in my optic nerves, behind my ears, in my palms lining my spine, on my breasts
Wind chime beneath my breath, what did you do to me?
There were turntables. Turntables. Turntables.
Turntables. Turntables.
Inescapable as your voice.

You've got the authority of an untamed lion prepared
to attack,
destroy, build,
populate,
uplift and
repeat.
I've got the
agility to get
past things as
water often
sneaks under
doors, seeps
through
cracks,
disguises
itself as mist,
gets absorbed
and explores
its host.
Nothing can
hide from us.
Nothing can deny our will.
Nothing could have undermined us,
Except each other.
Is it any wonder why
the nights still go peacefully unslept?

I once kissed a poem into your mouth. And I can still hear it every time you breathe out.

Fyre

Open letter to Mr. Fyre,

Dear old flame
Tonight my thirst writes
I'm hungry
Starvation has hollowed this body
Emptied these bones
I'm melting without marrow
Tomorrow will be no different than yesterday
Expansive as the night sky is
Its mass does not outweigh the first mouthful of dawn

As nice as sobriety may be
There will never be a state of mind
Sweeter than this supernatural high
Both metaphysical and cosmic
Love, I've been skywriting your name with my
fingertips
Hands still limp
Limbs lethargically standing loose
Seeking the refuge of your spine

Standing here
I'm still standing here
See me
Half a skeleton
Remembering those nights when we were clad in flesh
When everything clung to you by its fingernails and
The ends of the universe were right outside your door

The cracked edge of what had just begun to harden

Lingering on the tips of our tongues
Our mouths were
Two Mack trucks on a suicide mission
1000 miles per hour
Towards your face
We crashed
Sweating bones and salted brows

Exploding

We emitted universes and planets
Galaxies that expanded across your living room
This big bang never hid behind a theory

Enough truth to hurt just as bad as it was beautiful
Felt too good to last
And lasted too long to forget and walk away from.

People like us don't know how to fall
Only crash

Even when we see the ground is coming
We learn the choreography to gravity and
When we land
I'll still be playing cartographer
Across the map of your torso
Down your xylophone ribs

Then I'll find the Everest of your eyes as I start to
climb
I'll scale the ridges of your cheekbones
And lay hammock soft in the crescent

Of your right dimple

Yesterday
I heard cherry blossoms in your wishing well throat
Closing my eyes
I tossed my coined fragrance into the phone
Making a wish on the aroma of our conversation
Did you hear it?

I'm sorry.
I promised I wouldn't do this.
And I swear I didn't mean to wake you
It's just the tweaking monsters know your number
better than Anyone's

Four nights ago
Confession melted like sugar in your mouth
And now
I'm just wondering when.
When will you save me from the withdrawals?
The starving?
I am a lioness
I prey on you
Saying grace at a cannibal's dinner table

There is a hollow
Caught in my veins, liver, lung, gut, stomach
I am not whole

Should I wipe the songs from my tongue?
Try to forget?
Delete the numbered photographs
Or merely admit that I'm human

Lay my head against the dark wall of the confessional
And accept that I'm made whole in error and weakness
Made clean in broken?

I guess I'm just too damn good at wishing
Wishing you still held me like the sea holds her
sunrise
Wishing that I was still the one you kissed
Wishing I could be the melody to any love song that
made you Want to exist
We kissed like the universe could collapse on a bottom
lip
Like apples were the only fruits known to man
Like heaven and hell would crack and fall into on each
other
Unnatural and accidental
Like something you can't stop looking at

We kissed like the apocalypse
Lips
Train wrecked and deconstructed onto each other

Saying yes to you was an exercise in abandon
Saying no was an exercise in will
But I got about as much will as a junkie looking for
her next hit
So...in the sands of Beloved Neruda
Waves lapping hungry and wet at my feet
"Silent and starving I'll prowl through the streets
Bread does not nourish me
Dawn disrupts me
All night I will hunt for the liquid measure of your
steps

Until you find me"
Again

I still look for you in the planetary alignments.

Not Sex

I know. But we came close.
And if I'd had a body count it would've ended with you.
My virginity was wet for you. She sat at your feet while
we talked about music
and poetry, and light years, and oceans too far away to
map all the while focusing on how your lips moved.
What they would taste like
How they would feel pressed
against lips,
and lips.
I felt my hips widen as if something between me was
sizing you up.
Like a Python about to eat something larger than its
mouth, my body was preparing itself.
The longing hung in our space like cobwebs and dust,
and I know you were tired of sneezing.
But you still wouldn't take my offering.
So, naked, in the mirror, we stood eyes open. The four
of us were still and appreciative.
I know those two tore into each other on the other side
of that mirror.
Bet they laughed at our purity and wanted to show us
up.
They are probably still in love.
How tightly would you have fit into my body? Love,
once you made a home there,
would you have held onto me as you thrust and
trusted me to submit, open, hold tight, hold still, hold
you in...
Would my legs have become twine around your waist?
while your body, a passion spiked over in thorns,

fed into mine and plucked pleasure from the tips,
edges, slits, dips, curves
and moisture of things.
Would you have bitten me as hard as I would've asked
you to?
Maybe let me ride with my hands tied behind my back.
I would've liked it like that.
Would you have sucked at my breasts and held my
arms down firm enough to make me understand.
That this is the forever you have always talked about.
That this is where the full moon comes from.
In me is where you belong.
That this is where the tides find their inspiration to
lick at the toes of the shore.
Our sex: the next level of breathing.
Would you have come for me?
Panted my name into my ear three times before you
could no longer make out the syllables?
Would your sweat have tasted like sweet copper and
zinc and cherries?
How might you have used your tongue to distract me
from the pain of things stretching?
I would have let you crush and bend me into your own
personal pressed flower.
Something that lived in your bedroom. Wild. Feral.
And beautiful for only you.
Taken you into my mouth, and warmed the liquid
truth out of you.
Have you ever wondered what it would have tasted like
to have named me "mine" and only referred to me as
such?

I've got tattoos inside my vagina that spell your name backwards.
To remind my body that even though we've never been one in this life,
there is an astral plane where everything is opposite.
And in the opposite,
you undid me.

My love for you is a tattoo I got
when my heart was too drunk
to say no.

Fairview E6

Until you've seen his room hazy and cloudlike from the sleep in your eyes and the 6 AM sun.

Until he wakes you up kissing you before he leaves for work.

Tells you he'll scoop you after your last class.

Until you've shared food from the same plate even when there are plenty of plates to go around.

Until he pulls you from a circle of really pretty dancing girls and asks you to come with him.

And you become his private dancer behind the DJ booth, and he starts playing songs he knows your body knows the lyrics to.

Until you are shameless, unafraid, wild, and so irrational, you don't recognize yourself.

Until you try to tell him you are ready.

For what?

For everything.

And he won't go there with you, but still, won't let you go.

Until you hear him whispering beautiful things to you while he thinks you're asleep.

Until he slips a drink out of your hand in front of your friends because he knows you don't drink and wants to keep it that way.

Until you share a pillow, drool pooling before your faces and morning breath fellowshipping in the air between.

Until you sleep on his floor next to him after he's given up his mattress and you wrap yourself around him for warmth.

Until you throw him against the wall and order him to
love you.
Until he hickeys your neck for the first time and you
are sure you will die that day happy and lacking
nothing from life.
Until you bite into his lip and swallow the bit of blood
you draw by accident.
Until you need him.
Until people start expecting to see you over his house
and asking you what you two have to eat.
Until you start leaving things over there. A book, a hair
brush, a sweater, a pair of panties, another book.
Until you fall asleep on his couch with gum in your
mouth, and you spend the morning before he wakes
up trying to scrub it off, but he notices anyway
because you don't know how to get gum out of a
couch.
Until you wait for him on his porch like his puppy and
you're fine with that.
Until it's raining so hard the lights flicker and you're
nervous, but he doesn't know that you're mildly afraid
of the dark, yet somehow he knew you needed to be
held at that moment.
Until he starts reading your mind and you get so
freaked out you start reading the Bible again.
Until he turns on that song and you two Passa Passa
and eat fried plantains that morning until it's time for
you to go to class.
Until his apartment is more home than you have
known since you left your family.
Only then can you appreciate your own threshold for
pain when he tells you

WE

    Can't Do

       This

          Anymore.

Love and slavery are the same shade of chain silver

Raz Fyre

Giant pearl in the sky.

If it is an empty crescent she will go to bed alone, and hungry.

But if the moon is full, she will lace up her wings and impersonate an angel who was assigned to him. Fascination will hold him, hopefully.

She and the man that can read hieroglyphics have been dancing together for six years and still can't catch the beat to save their lives. But the full moon belongs to them.

She keeps his picture somewhere she can't see it; imagines its tender whisper using his voice to comfort her on those nights the music is violent, and she realizes she is dancing alone.

The man that can read hieroglyphics and spit poetry and prayer in Kemet, casted a spell on her so slow, so sweet, so absolute, so fresh, so devastating that language no longer found her tongue. There are parts of her that are still silent. Love in her that is still silent, unused, ruined.

Behind her eyelids hope waits to be strangled in pleas begging God to take him and the pain away from her house.

She wakes suddenly reaching across the empty bed grabbing at a him-shaped absence. Dead air has never weighed as much as a grown woman rolling off her bed on purpose to take her mind away from missing him.

She did that.

She thought she was crazy. She loved him before he said a word to her.

His words were half born babies awaiting her womb to exist. His word was fertilization, and she carried his children. Her poetic uterus expanded as the universe did to make room for life. Their first born's name was "Fyre".

"Fyre" was a poem that loved her daddy so much she scribbled his name in used notebooks and walls and bathroom stalls and on napkins, and she sang about him to audience upon audience. "Fyre" sang for her daddy some, but he didn't recognize her. She still cries for him as does her mother.

She thought she was crazy. Thought she had imagined the intimacy. Wasn't it intimacy? Car rides under black ocean painted in full moon, and half lust, but all love...Love, wasn't it intimacy?

"What have you done to me?" she asked silently. Language escaped her even then.

He kissed her so softly on that couch the first time; she thought she was sleeping. So deeply she thought the skin on her lips would fall away from her face like torn pages from a poem she was afraid to write. The light of the Moon silver polished them over, and they froze in time that morning...or night...or evening.

"Pull me in. Need me. Hold me. Keep me here keep me here keep me here. If you leave me now, I might die. I love you." she pled silently as he kissed her neck. Language escaped her even then.

There was no mercy in his body.

He was warm even when he was cold, and wore her around him proudly when he slept at night.

And if there ever was a drug that kept its victims unclean, it was in his breath. Suddenly oxygen didn't mean so much to her anymore.

Suddenly she needed affirmations. She needed to know why sometimes he spoke without looking at her and disappeared for days at a time. Needed to know why he didn't know why she was upset with his absence.

"Where are you? I will hunt. Where are you? I will bleed. Come back, come back, come back." She cried silently. Language escaped her even then.

She thought she was crazy. Started to think she'd overvalued an imaginary relationship as those succumbing to infatuation often did.

She retraced her steps and his words only to find that all that was left of them was a slow two-step.

This dance they do around each other, this tango neither of them wanted to be a part of because every time the music changed they'd wake up. Apart. Misunderstood. And alone.

The night she saw his laugh being deep-throated by another, the night his hands taunted her all the way down someone else's spine, the night she understood she'd lost him,

She finally went home.

She buried him.

Then she cut herself open to make sure his memory was no longer moving inside her

And she shut herself up for 37 days.

In those 37 days, she tried to make him become nothing to her as she had become nothing to him.

Baptized in grief, she still kept his picture somewhere she couldn't see it. But it was there. Always there, whispering.

I still look for you in the aftertaste of the evening I refuse to spit out. The saliva does not only belong to me.

37 days

I cannot eat.
My hair falls into plates of food untouched.
I touched myself to make sure I was still alive, still not sure.
Parts of me fall out every time I stand up, so I stay in bed most days .
In my head, most days,
I see his footsteps away from me like a warrior walking away from a battle still going on. There is still gunfire and blood splatter on tattered bed clothes. I don't change my clothes anymore.
Most days my body is not home, it is prison, and I'm scratching my way out of the skin. Floating right above myself, a formless entity that was never meant for love.
What do you do when you need to scrape things out of yourself, but you are unsure of what tools to use?
Do you experiment with drugs and liquor until your insides melt to a viscous pulp and wet your legs on their way out?
Do you end it quickly with the souvenir knife you took from his house that day you had Pancakes with apple butter and talked about how wack that "Paranormal Activity 2" movie was?
Do you watch that movie by yourself and cry until there's nothing left but ragged breath?
Do you call and hang up over and over until He calls you back and tells you to stop?
At least then he would call you right?
You've got to purify yourself again.
Get it together girl. You must get it together girl.
Girl...not woman.

If you were a woman, you'd take a shower.
You'd say a prayer and stable your legs like you got
some good sense.
You would talk to your grandmother. Fold your
grandfather's socks while she washes the greens for
Sunday dinner. You'd ask her to teach you to make
the sweetest sweet tea the south has ever seen.
You'd drink it like an anti-communion. (He hated
sweet tea.)
You'd pick green beans with your mother barefoot and
sing with her that hymn about your soul moving out of
your broken building of a body.
You'd smile at the hope in it.
You'd dance, fade in and out of reality. Smile too long
at people while only half listening.
You'd mask it and collect plastic for recycle to save the
world since you've already lost yourself.
Or, volunteer at a pet shelter where you could kiss the
kittens between their furry ears.
You'd wear shorts that didn't go past your knees, and
appreciate the looks from other men.
If you were a woman, you'd let yourself notice other
men without considering it betrayal to him.
He is not here to admire your new shorts.
You'd try your best not to stand on the rails of bridges
that sit above Tennessee Rivers waiting to swallow
you.
And perhaps you'd learn to swim just in case.
But you've had 37 days to stop being reckless with
yourself
to decide to be girl or woman.

Just remember, woman belongs to no one and gets on with her life.
But girl will ALWAYS be His.
And he will NEVER be hers.

I've always been your magnet
and although love is never
really magic...this time it was.

Honest Question

Why haven't you seen me?
Everyone else has.
Must've been a dream.

Pride?

A woman must always magnify herself.
Observe her own movement like microscopic life on a
slide, slide herself out of temptation.
Knows too well what it is.
To need to be noticed, but not dare ask for attention.
To try to be attractive to someone but careful not to
look like she's trying.
She must hang herself
In the balance between being mysterious and being
invisible.
And she is invisible. Today.
To the only one that matters.

It's like I swallowed an overachieving architect. Put my skyscraper heart back where you found it, Raz.

Red

The man who reads hieroglyphics
And casts shadows on Venus
And eats pomegranates with gold-leaf
And talks backwards
And studies soundwaves
And dreams in Kemet
Is tumorous and malignant
I was in love for 1095 days
Then I lost count
I do not know the man I love and I wonder if I ever did
I witnessed the man I love find his soulmate that
Spring
First April then May...then forever
He couldn't go a day without seeing her smile
And suddenly he no longer had to
Amen
No flowers grew for me
Even as I melted into the grass
Fertilizer
I prayed for him to rewind himself
Come back to me, remember me
To come into me
But it doesn't matter how many times you say grace
If you're sitting at a table with nothing to eat
I can't look at him
I hate the color red, the moon
and pancakes
and Pangaea
Broken as it is, and irreparable
Pangaea's body parts are timeless

Suddenly
The earth and I are sisters

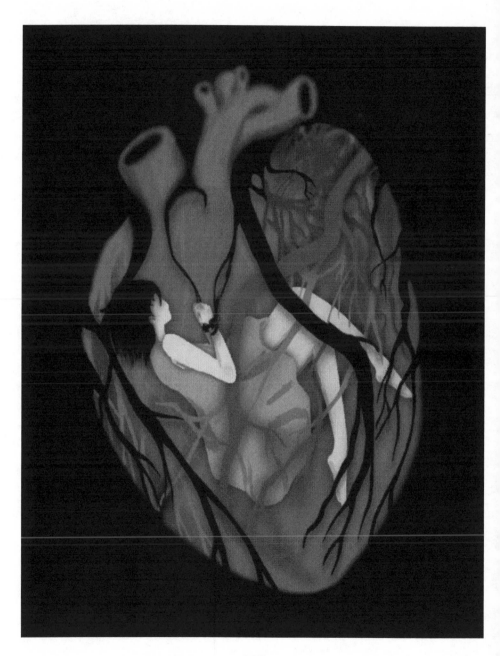

My bones still make a home beneath the dirt of your tombstone Lyric.

12/14/2011

When I withdraw from you
As do ghosts from the minds of the living
As my grief ebbs into a wet and monumental silence
As those tears shame my reflection
I will unlearn my capability of loving like an eclipse
I'll stop stitching shadows across my sun trying to
catch the moonlight
Of a Morning Son so bright he'd make Lucifer jealous

*But I would still follow you anywhere, baby. Even into
the fire.*

I will learn to stop giving my teeth to people
One by one until I'm smiling thru black window gaps
A broken version of what was there before
I know you didn't do it on purpose
And I know I'm not the only one that carries this
darkness
But
You make me carry it alone.
You make me watch you with my replacement
You come around
You make me pretend my ankles are sturdy enough to
carry me and this
Ache
You do not speak on this anymore
You smile
You act like I am made of stone
So I became a grinning boulder
Older than I should be on the inside
Trying to die from natural causes

You make me crazy
So when I withdraw from you
As a man trying not to spill seed into a womb that only
wanted pleasure
I will take my member and my orgasm with me
We
Were as anticlimactic as two could have been
Edging on explosion but never giving in
Our time together an armageddon that began as a
laugh in the night
Ended with a gurgling scream in the dark
What was on the other side of that door you wouldn't
let me open
Those tangled hours
Spent hanging on your words, lapping at the air for a
piece of your mind
Should all be forgotten
I suppose I should throw away what you mean to me
Accept my place as a drowned woman settled on the
floor of the sea
Eyes watching starfish
Unblinking
When I withdraw from you
The process will look something like a detox from
white powder
I will be unrecognizable as those good girls with bad
habits
Writhing to escape from themselves as their bodies beg
for more
I'll do a sickening twirl for you in my bed
Fetal position and shivering with fever, foaming at the
mouth

Am I still as beautiful as when you first said you loved
me?
This is what your love is on me
When you tell me, mine doesn't fit you
Or that you don't want it
So when I withdraw from you
As does God from a philosopher's understanding
As does understanding from a God that frowns upon
philosophy
When I finally withdraw
I will unlearn you, as I have unlearned my own fear
And cherry blossoms will grow
In the spot I lay in when I couldn't move
From beneath your music.

So when we collide and tangle
like sneaker laces, microphone
chords, and cheap Mardi Gras
necklaces don't run from me.

Apology

I'm sorry I fell so hard too,
but this is where we are now.
Do you remember when you told me to masturbate
until I was over you and happy again?
As if the fix was finite and simple like skin.

It has never been about sexual desire.
It will only ever be about you.
All of you.

You being consistent, you refusing to disappear,
You not resisting while pretending you don't feel.
You being present, even if not often.
Apologies are antidotes and antivenom,
Always appreciated, and aromatic as attars
But this is not about sorry either.
It is about change
And chains that just won't break.

Things said in fits of passion and protest of your absence:

"If I can't have him I might as well not be a woman."

Closure

There is no such thing as closure for people like us.
People that swear to meet each other on the other side.
The next lifetime is a lifetime away.
Closure? Is a human thing, and we've always spoken
like spirits only passing thru this shift, baby.

"You were the one for me." Saith He, my deity, with his eyes like fire, and his mouth like the first and sweetest taste of cocaine. Folding inward for his blessing, I accepted this truth. And that night was an afterlife worth dying for.

And then I was high.

Higher than a human ought to be.

The last time I felt
like this,
as old as a
hieroglyph,
you were teaching
me something
about death.

A Chant in Whispers

Who am I without you? I'm still in love with you. Who am I without you? Who am I without you? Who am I without you? Who am I without you? I have never not loved you. I do not love without you. I cannot love without you. I have never not loved you. Come into me. I have never not loved you. Hold me. I need you. Backup, I can't control myself. Let me touch you. Backup. Take me back. Don't push me away. I need you. Who am I? Who am I? I can't look at you right now. Hold me. Hold me. Hold me. Hold me. I thought you'd forgotten me. I wish you'd let me touch you. Why did you come back? Stay. Stay? Stay. Who am I without you? I will wait forever. Don't let me go. I will search for you in the next lifetime, baby. In the next lifetime. Next lifetime. Next lifetime. Next lifetime. Wait for me.

Yesterday, Tennessee Williams told me that the longest distance between two people is time.

Two Lantern Hearts Stumbled Irresponsibly in the Night

After a few tangos and a song of despair
The darkness threw itself at them
As things often do in the night.
Soon their love was blindness feeling around for itself.
Embarrassed and alone they parted towards their
respective sides of the earth.
Though bereft of passion
She led a normal life, barefoot, and distracted.
Full of passion but bereft of her
He observed the music of his life as one long
crescendo.
It sounded like her voice,
And made him want to cut his ears off
But at least it was music.
At least she'd left something behind.
At least they will always have the memory
of the tangoes
to live in

Epilogue

My heart's designated driver.
May all of our dehydration drown.

ADE'

"...you shall be together even in the silent memory of God,

But let there be spaces in your togetherness,

And let the winds of the heavens dance between you.

Love one another, but make not a bond of love

Let it rather be a moving sea between the shores of your souls."

–Khalil Gibran

Water

"What does it mean to be clean?" she asked, following him around his garden barefoot. And the man responded,
"Wash your feet before you step into someone's home...or life.
If you are offered bread, only take what you can hold in one hand, and do not eat until your host has joined you.
Give until your hands are empty.
Do not dance in the streets and expect reverence.
Keep your eyes open while you kiss
Do not kiss until you've drawn a map of your partner's life and you see yourself an island of his existence
Forgiveness is clean
Lean out of your window to wring the past from your hair
And keep company with only those who have seen you under both sun and storm."
That night she spent a squatter in his home.
 She pondered his wisdom and wrote of famine and eating. She was going to bear him a Son of lyric.
Dear dark watershed within,
I no longer break amen
And if there was a prayer as sweet as a poem
Skywritten and bathed in starry black, would you give
it back to me inside our intimacy?
Just as her writing was getting deeper,
becoming poetry trying to birth its way out of her system,
the man came in and ripped up her words.

Wiping the confusion from her brow, tucking her deep into the
beloved goose feather
he smiled,
"I don't need that from you. Why not just say what you mean? That is the definition of clean."

I carry you in the whites of my blood cells.

When I feel your palms, I feel the faces of our children.

Not Sex...

The man shows the woman his collection of beautiful objects.
"Over time, I've taken things from every corner of the earth, preserving their elegance with polish, salt, or formaldehyde. I keep them here forever to speak with pride of my experiences and status.
Some men do this with women.
I find it better to not carry people's shadows in my pocket."
Suddenly my clothes were not so heavy anymore.

I could not keep my hands quiet for needing to understand your flesh.

Grove 317

Until you have asked him, again and again, to stop it
with the affection,
You are not used to the warmth, and it makes you feel
unworthy.
Until you see him give the last money in his wallet to a
homeless person.
Until he tells you he wants to find God but does not
know where to look, so he tips in tithes and gives as
though he will die tomorrow.
Until he brings you to your family because you're
afraid to drive, and they treat him like a son.
Until you are sure he will leave you for how often you
cry these days, but all he does is listen, wipe tears,
watch movies, and repeat.
Until he is so patient with you, you start to trust his
hands more than he does.
Until you wake up to a kiss that ends your life.
Until you are reincarnated as his woman.
Until you eat pizza and watch cartoons while staring at
him.
Until he asks you why you're staring and you tell him
you are drawing a map of his life and naming your
island.
Until he tells you are so beautiful that it makes him
ache,
And you understand he's talking about the things
you're holding to your chest and not showing to
anyone but him.
Until he shines the swine off your pearls,
And makes those pearls into a crown.

Until he literally calls you "my Queen," daring you to
disagree.
Until he teaches you to drive at night
And later you make a home of heat vent and foggy
windows
Finding sleep
In the front seat.
Only then can you look at yourself in a mirror, peel
everything off
And trust yourself to want again.
And of course, you want again.
This time when you abandon yourself,
You are not as careful as you promised your reflection
you would be.
Because you are not the only one who seems to be
jumping off things.

24 hours

You kept me awake for 24 hours.
Woman, I had to go to work in the morning.
24 hours I've been awake little woman,
And you are wrapped up in my blanket, not sleeping
 Drinking my orange juice
Sitting here laughing into the night.
My little woman, loud and ridiculous and strange.
Do you see what time it is, or are you too busy
touching my face?
Drawing life from a little light and a little intimacy.
You don't care what time it is as you speak towards
the dark.
Some of the things you say have me wondering if I've
made a mistake.
But you make me forget when you treat my anecdotes
and advice as lyric.
Why do you listen so hard?
Love so hard?
Why do you bite down when you kiss and who taught
you to suck the blood from your lovers?
Little woman, where are you from?
I know you're sleepy, I can feel it in your breathing.
Drift off little woman and let me rest.
24 hours you've been telling the same joke,
Asking the same questions,
And touching my face,
And drinking my orange juice.

We met at the turn of the century.

Honest Response

If you asked me to marry you with a circle of tin foil
and a promise,
I would say yes.

Humility

There are certain instances where being exposed is not
cancerous
To a woman.
Instances where letting her guard dogs sleep
And letting the world happen to her.
Asking for exactly what she wants and getting it
Does not cheapen her.
Pride has no place between Ade' and his beloved.
In his consistency, she's never left to guess what fresh
hell might be brewing in his mind
If she were to unwind the prison wire from around her
love.
She never fears his leaving.
He never sees her desperate, but devoted.
Her nakedness to him is like his own.
She is no novelty but precious just the same.

I find you in the places I rest my eyes when phasing out. The Sun understands this.

On Absence

We fight because we love and we must stay in love
while we fight.

Fluorescent Gold

The man that understands the earth better than
master nature
And hung light bulbs behind weakened stars
And reads binary code
And writes in the language of robots
Is the man I cannot live without.

We were picking cherries, about to wash them for
dessert when I noticed how soft the air around him
went when we brushed hands.
Ade' does not hang the moon and does not spit out the
sun
Instead, he brings bread to the village children without
shoes, he gives food for thought to those degenerate
enough
To worship gold as God.

Ade' is a god that gives credit of creation to the womb
Even though I've seen him grow light out of his hands,
and feed a baby bird, and purify a creek by drinking
from it.
He doesn't know I know his secrets.
There is power in a compassionate man that is some
kind of futuristic king.

But he only uses that position to nurture.
"Will you clean these carrots for lunch?" he asks me,
unassuming as a simple farmer, straw hat and all.
I can't see much past this royalty, and I don't want to.
My favorite color is dark chocolate.

I love the smell of fresh rosebuds, brownies, honesty,
and lemons
And the Earth and I are not sisters after all;
She is my daughter.

8/22/2015

And the woman said
When I vow myself to you
I will tell the truth about an imperfect man
Falling his way towards an imperfect woman
His feet sturdy below his knees as he challenges her to
love
Like an eclipse.
Challenges her to show him her dark parts
So he can part the dark at the scalp and reveal to her
That even though her past might be nappy, it is
beautiful
And growing towards a universe
That has a future painted out starry verse and
Beloved blackness
Black love is
A representation of everything that holds these planets
in line
Black love is the belly of reason rhyme and time
And on this day we are its children
When I vow myself to you
As some do oaths written in blood
I will stop trying to understand what you see in me
Stop trying to decode the writings between God's
palms
And accept the gift
Psalms 85:10 Mercy and truth are met together;
righteousness and peace have kissed *each other.*
When we kiss each other
I leave my mouth in your hands
Whisper you a prayer song about how grateful I am

That we are the marriage between righteousness and
peace
We are the space between these notions
That people no longer sentence themselves to life
behind the bars of Someone else's ribs
The thing is
I am ready to commit to your bones,
Beloved I submit to making you whole
Though you are a finished work of art, I'm the part
The painter added to make us masterpiece.
And the man said
I will adorn your head with a crown of Calendula
This African marigold has a reputation
She opens up the sun and closes it at sunset
She has been crushed into Egyptian medicine since
the beginning of Time
My bride
You do not know your own power
And though you've made a home of my bones
Consider yourself the ruler of my spine
I will love you as Christ loved his church
Treat you with consideration of a delicate vessel
As I cherish my own ventricle and vessel
Heart and lung
Keep these prayers of thanks on my tongue
I will care for you with sacrifice, humility, and
Corinthian love
And the voice of fate speaks:
"you were born together, and together you shall stay
you shall be together even in the silent memory of God,
But let there be spaces in your togetherness,
and let the winds of the heavens dance between you.
Love one another, but make not a bond of love

Let it rather be a moving sea between the shores of your souls."
–Khalil Gibran

Sex!

It is not lyrical; it's spiritual.
Your body is not scroll for my finger painted escape
into metaphor.
You're not the paint I plunge index and middle into to
create things past realness.
However; here we are,
two fingers in
a slow breath out.
The pain of pleasure is as arresting as the sound.
Honey and desire dripped from your mouth
this substance made the entrance easier as you
untightened the hold my vagina had on keeping itself
modest
oh...but that was only the first time.

Before this desirous tide of new sexuality
now...

Take. Eat...Devour my body in this garden of you.
You kiss me like you're angry
and hold me down like quicksand.
You love slow like overturned secrets.
Delicious powerlessness worships in your climactic
chapel
I'll never crawl away.
I'll stay still on my knees...or prostrate
In observance of this expansive spastic crashing
This drastic passion your body is capable of.

You kiss me like you're angry, and I need that.
I need you,

sword and temper ...fire and snake bite,
lion's den.
I need fangs and flesh.
Your tongue is a flogger.
Lash me open. Empty. Suck everything out until my
terrain is to your liking then
Feel me....fill me
Take. Eat. This is how it will always feel. I am a
permanent indulgence.
Yet.
Still.
As fragile as the day
You first lay beside me and asked me if I was ready,
Ade'
Until the day when there are no more days
And we prepare for the aliens to shift our way of life
I'm here in your bedroom,
A wild, strange, pretty thing,
Pressed and preserved,
Only for the man, that planted these gardens.

Apology

Do you remember the time that silence was the reason
we almost didn't make it?
Communication, a science that escaped the rotation of
our voices.
Risen in anger tossing "no" back and forth like a hot
coal.
Praise the burn marks and teeth that learn to speak.
Praise the patience, empathy, and
Homeopathy of apology.
I'm sorry, my love.

Did you know you spun Saturn in your sleep? I saw you do it.

You were manna and, I couldn't fill my face fast enough.

Awake

When we fall asleep together for the last time
Everything will become as simple as two temperate
skulls
Grinning inside the earth
Keeping good company
Laughing the darkness away
Living inside the earth
Above the hearth of her soft, soil pocket
there will lay bouquets of things we left behind
The flowers will echo our story in a fresco of variation
Every color will become our favorite color
We will lie beneath the rainbow
While not knowing it as the rainbow
A mercy and a promise to have this everlasting rest
No flesh
But still in love.

We were royal and fat, but we provided our own feast.

A Song in Harmony

The sun rises, and we say yes. The sun opens, and we
say yes. Things go wrong, and we say amen. They do
us harm, and we say amen. Our feet bleed, and we
dance near the candelabra. The rain purifies, and we
open our mouths skyward. Things grow beneath our
fingernails, and we sow trees with our bare hands. The
sky is soundless, and we stay close to the sea, close
enough to see our reflective crossed lifelines on palm.
The clouds separate and the holes in between them,
from open eyes we stare back. When night comes back
and everything goes black we say amen and go to
sleep....do it again and go back to sleep.

Two Tired Time Travelers

Two tired time travelers meet for the 6078th time
during the 21st century while in the dimension with all
the humans in it.
This time, he is a computer programmer,
And she is a teacher.
Both thinking this is the only life they have ever and
will ever live
(As they have thought 6,077 times before)
They are careful,
until the moment a rose touches her lips
And those same petals touch his.
After that, there's nowhere else for either of them to go,
But together,
Into ever after.

Epilogue

Until death do us part.

ABOUT THE AUTHOR

Jacquelyn Swift is a performance poet. She is an MFA Creative Writing candidate at Sewanee University, and a former NAACP ACT-SO National Silver medalist in playwriting. By day she functions undercover as a Librarian, Bookmobile Librarian, a teacher, and the young bride of an insane computer genius. Under the cloak of night, she prowls thru the cities of Southeastern Tennessee in search of the nearest open mic or cypher to crash and burn a hole into someone's stage. In addition to her self-help poetry book "Monsters," Swift further expands her double life as a poet by teaching people how to find their stage legs as well as how to find their voice on paper through her workshop series "Fangs: Take a Bite out of your Stage Fright."